An Ohioan's Odyssey:
Lessons in Leadership, Law, and Public Service

John J. Kulewicz

Gibraltar Publishing Company LLC

john.kulewicz@gmail.com
614-364-5456

Cover image courtesy of *Columbus Citizen*, Grandview Heights Public Library, *Columbus Citizen-Journal* and *Columbus Citizen* Newspapers Collection.

ISBN-13: 979-8-9990709-0-6 (hardcover)
ISBN-13: 979-8-9990709-1-3 (softcover)
ISBN-13: 979-8-9990709-2-0 (ebook)

To Maryline and Adam and Abigail,
who mean everything to me.

Table of Contents

Foreword

An odyssey is a long journey, with a continuing flow of adventures and challenges. In American literature, no vein is richer than that of the self-directed journey. The open road. The test of mental and physical capacity. The acceptance of risk in search of reward. In *An Ohioan's Odyssey*, John Kulewicz, a descendant of Polish, English, and German immigrants, has made a valuable contribution to the genre.

From his competitive ocean swims to an argument in the US Supreme Court on health-care coverage, from managing Gary Hart's 1984 Ohio presidential campaign to seeking elective office himself, Kulewicz has found success through relentless effort, imagination, and preparation to overcome risk. With gratitude for the inherited blessings of family, his mentors in law and public service, and his immediate family, Kulewicz pays it forward by sharing valuable life lessons with grace and integrity.

During four decades at *The Columbus Dispatch*, I witnessed Kulewicz's commitment to and engagement in the civic and political life of our community and state. His attention to detail, insatiable desire to learn, and dedication to the common good have always been apparent in the public arena. What was not apparent to me, until reading this book, is the fusion of forces—intellectual, physical, and spiritual—that fuels his interior life, and thus, his extraordinary odyssey.

Whether stargazing atop Mount Kilimanjaro or reflecting on a particularly literate sermon from a London church pew, Kulewicz never ceases to nourish his spirit of discovery. As he enters the eighth decade of his life, that indomitable spirit undoubtedly will propel him to fresh adventures and challenges.

"Only the impossible is worth the effort," wrote English author Jeannette Winterson. That sentiment, Kulewicz confides, "has guided me as long as I can remember."

The road ahead beckons.

Michael F. Curtin
Former Editor
The Columbus Dispatch

Pronunciation Note

"How do you say that?" is a question that often arises when someone sees my last name for the first time. As with other Polish surnames, the pronunciation has been Americanized in the United States. In Eastern Europe, Kulewicz is commonly pronounced as "koo-LEV-ich." In America, it sounds like "COOL-uh-wits."

Whichever way you want to say it, I'm cool with that.

John J. Kulewicz

Preface

I have written this book for three reasons. It is meant primarily to encourage anyone looking for advice about life to know it is possible to imagine yourself into accomplishments that might first seem unattainable, to caution the reader to watch out for artificial impediments we sometimes impose upon ourselves, to vouch for the proposition that it is worth the effort to pursue goals that capture our imagination, and to give assurance that it is rewarding to live the life we dare to dream. The book may also serve as a reference for anyone who wants to know more about me, unworthy as I would be of such attention. Finally, it will be a repository of family information that otherwise might be lost to history.

I am indebted to my grandparents and parents for documents and stories they preserved; to my brothers, sister, cousins, colleagues, and friends for memories they have shared; and to my wife and children for the care they have given this manuscript. I likewise am obliged to the many people with whom I have shared experiences described in this book. In most instances, I have minimized the use of specific names out of respect for privacy and concern for inadvertent exclusions. In addition, compliance with the Ohio Rules of Professional Conduct has required me, as a lawyer, to maintain confidentiality of certain client information. I have taken care to confirm the accuracy of information in this book but assume full responsibility for any errors.

Omissions are also my responsibility. Even if it were possible to present an exhaustive account of a life that now spans seventy years, such a book would tax the patience of any reader. Streamlining is necessary to serve the purposes, noted above, for which I have prepared this book. By far, the hardest part of writing this book has been the discipline of omitting the names of literally hundreds of people whose guidance has shaped me and whose friendship I cherish. As readers likewise will understand, many personal details are better left personal. No omissions, however, affect the authenticity of the stories this book tells.

Preparation of a book like this gives an author much reason to be humble. Candid reflection on any life experience makes one recognize not only successes and accomplishments but also failures and shortcomings. What Eugene V. Debs once told a judge seems to me to strike the right chord: "Your Honor, years ago, I recognized my kinship with all living beings, and I made up my mind I was not one bit better than the meanest on Earth." In that spirit, and with hope that the book will serve the purposes for which I have written it, I thank you, the reader, for your consideration.

John J. Kulewicz
Columbus, Ohio
May 2025

Introduction

It was the day before my first argument in the Supreme Court of the United States. I was excited and confident but feeling the weight of the case. The resources for health-care coverage of over 157 million Americans were at stake, depending on how the court would interpret a key Medicare statute. Sitting alone in the back of a taxi on the crowded streets of Washington, DC, at the end of February 2022, I had a low moment as tough questions I expected to face the next morning overwhelmed me.

Unaware of my silent predicament, the driver started telling me her life story. She explained how important it was for her to count her blessings. Every day, she just counted her blessings. That simple reminder snapped me out of my momentary despair and cleared my mind of anxiety and fear. I instead remembered the many strengths of our position and how lucky my client, colleagues, and I were to present the case to the Supreme Court.

Bolstered by months of preparation, the argument flowed well the next morning. The Supreme Court decided the case in my client's favor a few weeks later, and the health-care system avoided an expensive hit.

The driver's timely words of wisdom were one of many blessings that have come my way over the years. Among those blessings, I learned from my family early in life that success depends largely upon effort, imagination, and the confidence to take risks. I hope I am measuring up to the expectations of those who brought me into the world and, with my wife Maryline, providing the same opportunity for our son and daughter, Adam and Abigail.

With gratitude to the anonymous taxi driver and all others to whom I owe much thanks, I am honored to share with you in these pages many blessings I am fortunate to count. It has made a huge, positive difference in my own life to count my blessings rather than dwell on my shortcomings. I hope this book will prompt anyone who reads it to find in their own blessings the same opportunity to live the lives they dare to dream.

Chapter 1: Origins

I am the fortunate descendant of grandparents and parents who strived all their lives so their families could flourish.

My Paternal Grandparents: Joseph Kulewicz and Josephine Kogut

My paternal grandfather, Joseph Alexander Kulewicz, was Polish. He was born on March 19, 1894, in Skorvody, a small town with no running water. It is now in the Republic of Belarus, whose border with Poland has shifted over the years, but was under Russian control at the time of his birth. His father died when he was three. Joseph's high school graduation certificate classified him as "a peasant of the Roman Catholic faith" and certified in September 1909 that he had completed two years of study at the Zhirmunsk People's Academy in the nearby town of Lida. A little over four years later, shortly before he turned twenty, he left Skorvody unannounced. His mother learned about Joseph's departure after the fact, when he sent her some money.

Joseph obtained a passport in Libau (now in the Republic of Latvia), the port city from which thousands of central European émigrés were then departing for the United States. He boarded a ship for New York early in 1914, shortly before the outbreak of the Great War, now known as World War I, in central Europe. After his arrival on Ellis Island, Joseph went to New Castle, Pennsylvania, where a cousin was living. He found a job there as a sheet metal worker at the American Sheet & Tin Plate Company.

In June 1917, two months after the United States entered the war, Joseph registered for the military draft. His registration card specified that his mother was solely dependent on him for support. He enlisted as a private in the United States Army in September 1917, in the Eleventh Company, Third Battalion, of the 165th Depot Brigade. The unit was responsible for organizing incoming recruits, outfitting them with uniforms and equipment, and conducting their basic training. He served in that capacity at Camp Travis near San Antonio, Texas, and received an honorable discharge in December 1918, when his unit demobilized at the end of the war.

After his discharge, Joseph eventually settled in Martins Ferry, Ohio, a town on the Ohio River. Martins Ferry was one of the first settlements founded in Ohio after the opening of the Northwest Territory in the late eighteenth century. During the Industrial Revolution of the late nineteenth and early twentieth centuries, it became a coal-mining and steel-producing center in which many Central and Eastern European immigrants found jobs.

There, Joseph was a member of the Polish National Alliance and one of the founding members of the Polish Club in 1923. He became a naturalized citizen of the United States the next year. He worked in several steel mills and factories. His job in the Sheet Metal Department of the Jones & Laughlin Steel Company required him to wear special shoes because he had to use his feet to separate tin out of the furnace. When the company closed, Joseph went to Chicago for a year to work as a janitor. Returning to Martins Ferry, he took a job as a custodian and millworker at the Wheeling Steel Corporation.

Years later, people who had worked in the mills, factories, and mines during that era reminisced about the plight he and other workers had faced. "You'd show up every morning just outside the plant," they would tell me, "and the foreman would look over the crowd, calling, 'I'll take you, I'll take you, I'll take you.' If he didn't pick you," they lamented, "you'd earn nothing that day." It was a highly vulnerable way to try to make a living and support a family. Collective bargaining and unionization took strong root in such a one-sided environment. Joseph was a member of the United Steelworkers of America.

By the mid-1940s, he earned enough to buy a two-story home on North Fifth Street in Martins Ferry, complete with multiple bedrooms and bathrooms, a full standard kitchen, a sunroom, a coal-fired furnace, and an outdoor entryway into the cellar. It was a long way from Skorvody, literally and figuratively, and fitting for the imagination of a "peasant of the Roman Catholic faith" who had boldly left his small hamlet just decades before with little but hope to his name.

Joseph returned once to his birthplace, in May 1931, crossing the ocean aboard the *SS Kościuszko*. The rest of his branch of the Kulewicz family had remained in Skorvody. Fighting between Soviet and Nazi forces during World War II caused the family to take refuge often in the nearby woods. The woods again became a sanctuary during the Stalin era of communist control that followed. Joseph's brother Boleslaw had stayed in Skorvody with his wife and children. The fact that Joseph was living in the United States put Boleslaw "on the Siberia list as a suspected spy," his daughter Bernarda recalled. A friend would alert Boleslaw whenever the police were coming to pick him up, at which point he would go to the woods. By 1958 Boleslaw and his family decided they no longer wanted to stay in the Soviet Union. They relocated to a part of southern Poland ceded from Germany after World War II, leaving the small town from which Joseph had departed over forty years earlier.

When Joseph moved to Martins Ferry after his wartime service, he met Josephine Kogut, another member of the Polish émigré community. Her mother ran a boarding house in which he was renting a room. The daughter of Ignaz "Eli" Kogut and Mary Federman Kogut, Josephine was born on August 19, 1904, in Dąbrowa, a town in southern Poland near Kraków.

Josephine had come to the United States as a young girl with her family in 1912. The family lore is that Josephine and her family originally had tickets for passage aboard the *Titanic*. But as her brother Rudolph Kogut told me, their father "had a little problem with his eyes, and they were held back at the dock because he didn't pass his physical." Rudy concluded, "We were lucky. We wouldn't be here if we had caught that ship." As third-class passengers, presumably, it is almost certain they would have been trapped in the ship when it went down on April 15, 1912. Records date Josephine's arrival in the United States as May 30, 1912, aboard the *SS President Lincoln*, after which she went to Martins Ferry. Josephine became a naturalized citizen twenty-eight years later, in September 1940.

Joseph and Josephine married on October 22, 1921. My father, Stanley Joseph Kulewicz, was born in their apartment on Lombard Street, near the banks of the Ohio River, on July 28, 1923. His sister, Stella Mary Kulewicz, followed two years later.

Josephine was a strong woman. Having lived through the Great Depression, she became very frugal. She would save paper napkins from restaurants for the rest of her life, even amid the relative comfort of her later years. Before she was married, Josephine worked at Imperial Glass. She listed her occupation as "housewife" on her naturalization application but during World War II worked as a laborer at the Martins Ferry factory of Wheeling Steel. Her work ethic was such that she continued to work for other employers until well into her eighties. Among her last jobs was housekeeping at the rectory of St. Mary's Catholic Church in Martins Ferry, several blocks away from her home. Martins Ferry is a hillside town situated in a river valley, yet she always walked and was still carrying heavy loads up and down the hill as an octogenarian.

She was also an extraordinary cook of Polish foods. Her cabbage rolls (*gołąbki*) set the standard for me. When my cousins and I were youngsters and showed up at her kitchen early in the mornings, she would welcome us with cups of coffee to which she added extra helpings of sugar. If the coffee did not wake us up, she would suggest we hold our wrists under cold water at the kitchen faucet. In the summers she made apple pies fresh from the trees in her backyard. She spoke English well but seemed more comfortable when conversing in her native Polish with my father and others.

Joseph and Josephine lived in Martins Ferry for the rest of their lives. Joseph died from colon cancer at age sixty-four in the early morning hours of November 13, 1958, when I was four years old. My father woke me up, kneeling beside my bed in tears and saying, "My father has just died." His death was the first I remember, a memory underscored by my recollection of seeing him in his casket at the funeral home, surrounded by banks of flowers. Decades later, it astounds me to page through the funeral home visitation book in which hundreds of people in his small town signed their names—a hallmark of an age of close-knit communities.

Josephine lived almost thirty more years, until May 31, 1987. The demise of the Industrial Revolution had taken its toll on Martins Ferry by then. The once-thriving town of hardworking people had lost many jobs. Closed businesses and vacant homes dotted many streets. The funeral home at which her family and few surviving contemporaries gathered for the visitation was one of the more active establishments in town. The economic decline of her surroundings did nothing, however, to diminish her legacy as a mother and grandmother and the success of the lives she and Joseph had made for themselves and their family in America.

My Maternal Grandparents: John Tuggle and Clara Neuer

My maternal grandparents were Clara Neuer Tuggle and John Hesco Tuggle. Clara was born in Cincinnati on June 19, 1901. Her family had German roots, a heritage of which Clara remained fond throughout her life, using German words and phrases with increasing frequency as the years passed. The predominantly Germanic population of Cincinnati provided a hospitable environment for the émigrés of the Neuer family.

Clara worked throughout her life in a variety of jobs. They included civil service positions with the US Department of the Army, work as a dietitian helper at a hospital, employment with the Wright Aeronautical Corporation, and many years as a homemaker. Upon her retirement from the federal civil service, the commanding officer of the United States Army Adjutant General School Center at Fort Benjamin Harrison in Indianapolis wrote to Clara to commend her "for the excellent service you have rendered" and wished her success in her retirement from a civil service career that "I am sure has been a source of pride to you." Her life at home and in the workplace gave Clara a sweet disposition that coexisted with a skeptical temperament. She died on January 5, 1988.

John Tuggle was born in Williamsburg, Kentucky, on August 25, 1901. A descendant of Englishmen who came to America in the seventeenth century, he was a diligent and industrious man throughout his life. From age fifteen until shortly before his enlistment in the military, he worked at Harlan Hospital in Harlan, Kentucky. His responsibilities were to "keep the hospital clean; help take the dead to the morgue; serve the bedfast patients; take care of the bed pans; keep the operation room cleaned up; keep the instruments sterilized."

He served from October 1919 through March 1922 as a private in Company F of the Fifth Infantry of the US Army, landing on the French shore in Brest in November 1919, a year after the armistice had ended the war. He departed from Andernach in Germany in March 1922, and received his honorable discharge two months later. He then briefly took a job as a telephone lineman in Wofford, Kentucky.

John returned to Europe in the summer of 1922, aboard the *Susquehanna*, to visit Antwerp in Belgium and study music in Coblentz, Germany, for a year. He arrived back in the United States on June 15, 1923, aboard the *George Washington*.

John Tuggle and Clara Neuer married the next year, on July 16, 1924. My mother, Marian Frances Tuggle, was their first child, born on June 14, 1925, in Cincinnati. She had a younger sister named Eileen, who was born two years later.

John progressed through a series of jobs, from conductor on the Cincinnati Street Railway to grocery clerk and grocery manager at a Kroger store in Cincinnati, grocery manager for the Atlantic & Pacific Tea Company, wholesale cookie seller, sales supervisor for Gilt Edge Bakery Products, and vice president and sales manager for a cookie factory in Indianapolis. His early entry into the workforce had been a matter of necessity. He later lamented that he had been sent to live with his father and stepmother, who largely ignored his needs and took advantage of his labor, when his parents split up when he was nine years old. He was essentially on his own until age sixteen, when, as he later wrote, "I was big enough to stand on my own two feet and make my way the best I could through this world without an education and no parents to help you."

Deprived of parental love, he reflected, "God has guided me all through my life. He gives me the strength and will to do when he said to me you are old enough and strong enough to deliver yourself from your father and stepmother whom has used you as a slave and made you do a man's work from the time you were ten until this moment." He recalled that one day, "as I was going along through the woods [to chop firewood for his stepmother], God came into my mind again and said, 'Johnnie there is a stump. Stick your ax in it and go to your mother.' And so that is what I did, and that is the way I got out of slavery."

Five years later, in an October 1967 letter, he affirmed that "it has been only by the will of God that I have been able to raise two fine daughters and they gave me four fine grandsons [this was two months before the birth of my sister Susan, his granddaughter] for my labors, patience and trust in God." He reiterated those values shortly before the end of his life, in a May 1979 letter to my mother, in which he wrote, "you and Stanley shure [sic] have a lot to be proud of. You all did a fine job. We did the best we could," he said by comparison. "My means were always so small that we did not progress very much."

After his daughter Eileen was killed in an automobile accident in December 1963, he retired in order to spend two years helping to raise my cousin Mike Roof until Mike's father married again. John and Clara subsequently sold the trailer in which they were living in Indianapolis for $2,500, taking a $3,400 loss, and moved to a small apartment "with enough furniture to get by with" while he went back to work for four hours a day "to pay rent and other bills."

John died of prostate cancer on October 16, 1979. He wistfully told my mother he thought he "had not made much" of himself, evidently oblivious to the sterling values he had passed on to his family by steadfast example.

And he underestimated the effect of his thriftiness. Grandma and Grandpa Tuggle left savings bonds for my brothers and sister and me in an amount that enabled each of us to make the down payments on our first homes.

My Parents: Stanley Kulewicz and Marian Tuggle

The paths of the Kulewicz and Tuggle families converged in Athens, Ohio, when Stanley Kulewicz and Marian Tuggle met at Ohio University at a dance. They married on May 16, 1953, at St. Mary's Catholic Church in Martins Ferry. I was born ten months later, on March 22, 1954, in Indianapolis, Indiana, where they were living after their marriage. My parents named me John Joseph Kulewicz after my grandfathers, John Tuggle and Joseph Kulewicz. I was their firstborn and was followed by my brother Thomas in 1958, my brother Stanley Jr. in 1959, and my sister Susan in 1967. My baptism took place on April 18, 1954, at St. Andrew the Apostle Catholic Church in Indianapolis.

My mother in her wedding gown, May 1953. (Photo by Gruber Studios, Wheeling, WV.)

My father's memories and experiences of his childhood were a formative part of my own early upbringing. Baptized into the Roman Catholic Church as Stanislaus Kulewicz three weeks after his birth, he grew up in Martins Ferry, where he attended elementary school (grades one through eight) at St. Mary's School and secondary school at Shreve High School (now known as Martins Ferry High School), from which he graduated in June 1942. Stanley had a variety of part-time jobs during his school years, including work as a newspaper carrier for the Polish daily newspaper *Dziennik Polski* and a job at Leo Clothier.

War was plainly on the horizon for him upon graduation from secondary school. Events around the world ultimately brought World War II to the doorstep of the United States during his high school years. The coordinated German and Russian invasion of Poland beginning on September 1, 1939, was engraved in his memory, as was the steady spread of war in Europe and throughout the Pacific region. The Japanese surprise attack on Pearl Harbor, Hawaii, on December 7, 1941, plunged the nation into full-fledged war midway through his senior year. The inside cover page of his 1942 high school yearbook, *The Ferrian*, bears his neatly stenciled inscription "Remember Pearl Harbor."

After graduating from high school and while waiting for the inevitable draft (the United States having declared war against Japan and Germany in December 1941), he worked at the Wheeling Steel plant in Yorkville, Ohio; in a machine shop in Martins Ferry; and as an airplane maintenance technician at Wright Patterson Airfield near Dayton, Ohio. In his technician role at the air base, he assisted in "over-hauling and servicing airplane engines, accessories, and propellers" and "repaired and reconnected instruments, ignition, and fuel and oil lines between engine and ship."

Upon receiving his draft notice, he reported for duty at the Fort Hayes Induction Center in Columbus, Ohio, on March 4, 1943, a date likewise embedded in his memory and often repeated to us. His basic training took place in St. Petersburg, Florida, followed by a sixteen-week airplane

11

maintenance school in Amarillo, Texas, and further training in Fort Myers, Florida (a six-week course in aerial gunnery); Harlingen, Texas (a two-week refresher course in aerial gunnery); and Riverside, California. Along with instruction in airplane mechanics, he received training in the use of .50-caliber machine guns.

Thus prepared, Stanley served as a technical sergeant and gunner in the United States Thirteenth Air Force, known as the Jungle Air Force due to the focus of its missions on islands of the South Pacific. The point of embarkation from the US mainland was Salinas, California. Service in the South Pacific took him through Honolulu, Johnston Island, Kwajalein in the Marshall Islands, Tarawa in the Gilbert Islands, Guadalcanal in the Solomon Islands, Borneo, the Philippines, and Guam. He and his crewmates were based in New Guinea, which was a staging area for the liberation of the southern Philippines from the Japanese occupation forces. The primary focus of their missions was the bombardment of oil and other supplies the Japanese were storing.

The crew fought in the battles of New Guinea, the southern Philippines, and Borneo. They flew a B-24 heavy bomber, on which they bestowed the name *Old Iron Ass*. The bombs weighed three hundred to five hundred pounds apiece. "It was dangerous," my father recalled. "You were like a flying gas station." When the plane was airborne, he was a top turret gunner with a .50-caliber machine gun, with the additional responsibility of monitoring the fuel gauge and making mechanical repairs in the event of an emergency. His military records state that, as a flight maintenance gunner, he "assisted pilot in operation of multiple-engined airplane by maintaining a constant check on its mechanical functioning. Fired serial machine guns in combat. Flew 26 missions. Noted readings of engine and navigation instruments. Maintained log of engine performance. Made limited repairs and mechanical adjustments while in flight." In his separate role as an airplane and engine mechanic, he was responsible for examining "portions of plane such as wings, fuselage, and stabilizers for evidence of damage and made minor repairs."

My father (seated) with his crewmates in the South Pacific, ca. 1944–1945.

Over the course of his service, he was decorated with three Bronze Stars and the Air Medal. The commanding general, George C. Kenney, one of the architects of the successful campaign in the Pacific Theater, wrote to his mother in Martins Ferry on July 20, 1945, as the war neared its victorious conclusion. He explained to her, as he explained to parents of other medal recipients, that the Air Medal "was an award made in recognition of courageous service to his combat organization, his fellow American airmen, his country, his home, and to you." General Kenney recounted, "Your son took part in sustained operational flight missions" that included "bombing missions against enemy installations, shipping, and supply bases, and aided considerably in the recent successes in this theater." By "doing just such things as that here in the Southwest Pacific," wrote the general, "your son and the sons of other American mothers" made "a very real and very tangible contribution to victory and to peace." He concluded, "I would like to tell you how genuinely proud I am to have men such as your son in my command and how gratified I am to know that young Americans with such courage and resourcefulness are fighting our country's battles."

My father received his honorable discharge in November 1945, two months after the Japanese surrender ended hostilities. Nearly sixty-five years later, my brothers and sister and I accompanied him to Resurrection Cemetery in Columbus to visit our mother's grave in the plot in which he, too, eventually would be buried. He saw on a nearby tombstone the engraved recognition of the decedent's service in World War II. He pointed to it and said, "I want that on my tombstone too." He passed away shortly afterward, six months after our mother, on May 20, 2010. Chiseled into the tombstone above his name are the words "US Army Air Forces WWII."

As a bugler played "Taps" after the veterans' honor guard presented me the folded flag that had covered his casket, my thoughts on the brilliant sunny morning of his funeral and burial drifted to the South Pacific and the military service of which he was so quietly proud. Bringing his life full circle, his sister (my Aunt Stella Otto) and one of his nephews (my cousin Matt Otto) handed me a canister of soil I had asked them to bring from the gravesite of Joseph and Josephine Kulewicz in Martins Ferry. A scoopful at a time, tossed in by each family member and friend who had come to the cemetery, it became the first earth to fill his own grave. When we went back to the family home after the burial service, my cousins brought the events of that emotional morning to a fitting close by bringing out a large flask and leading us all in a toast to the airman and family patriarch whom we had just laid to rest.

* * *

One of my earliest memories of my father is a conversation he and I had about his wartime service one morning at breakfast. I could not have been more than three or four years old. We were living in a rented two-story duplex in Grandview Heights, Ohio, a suburb adjacent to Columbus. Sitting with me at a table downstairs, he talked about life in the air as a crew member and on the ground in the jungle. It seemed larger than life. Not until sixty years later, when several teammates and I went to the South Pacific for a swim I organized in the Solomon Islands, did I realize how formative his overseas military service had been for my father, who had joined the armed forces less than a year after graduating from high school in the small town in southeastern Ohio he had rarely left.

His military experience proved to be formative for our entire family. People who have served in the military seem to develop a heightened sense of discipline, which they bring home with them. In the context of our family, that characteristic showed itself in frequent reminders to keep our shoes shined, not waste food, show up on time, cut loose strings from new clothing, and be prepared. It is not just people in the military who follow such rules, of course, but military service made precision a prominent characteristic of his personality.

The biggest effect the military had on my father was the opportunity it gave him for a college education. He was the first member of his family to go to college. As a veteran of World War II, he benefitted from the Servicemen's Readjustment Act of 1944, commonly known as the GI Bill, which President Franklin D. Roosevelt signed into law on June 22, 1944. It provided veterans with funds for a college education, unemployment insurance, and housing. By virtue of the GI Bill, he enrolled at Ohio University in February 1946. He studied business administration, with a specialty in accounting, and graduated on February 5, 1949, with a bachelor of science in commerce.

The decision to go to college required him to go beyond the comfort and constraints of his circumstances. The blue-collar community in which he had grown up was largely composed of first-generation immigrants from Central and Eastern Europe. Many of the residents had never finished grade school. I remember that one of his uncles once jokingly referred to him as "Joe College," which was probably meant in a lighthearted way but (from the tone) may also have been intended to convey the skepticism and occasional resentment sometimes faced by those who seek to improve upon their situations.

* * *

My mother's journey to college was different. She had grown up in the busy and sophisticated urban environment of Cincinnati, Ohio, and several of its suburbs (including College Hill, North College Hill, and Norwood). She ever after thought highly of Cincinnati, measuring most other cities against it (usually unfavorably), and had many pleasant memories of her childhood there, including trips to the Coney Island water park and her selection to compete in the Miss Cincinnati contest at the Hotel Gibson. She attended Norwood High School and Hughes High School and was proud long afterward of the academic caliber of each school. At Hughes High School, in addition to her studies, she was an active member of the drum majorette squad, receiving a letter in band for her participation.

In the middle of her senior year, she moved with her parents and sister to the small town of Washington Court House in rural southwestern Ohio. The adjustment was not easy. It took the efforts of a school administrator to prevail upon her to enroll in Washington High School and finish her secondary school education. That routine outreach proved to have enormous, positive consequences for my brothers and sister and me decades after the fact. Without that push, our mother may never have finished high school and would not have been able to enroll in college afterward. She likely would never have met my father and joined with him in having four children, all of whom are college graduates.

As I was growing up, my mother had strong views on the importance of education, which she readily expressed to my brothers and sister and me. Her personal history attested to the priority she placed on education. Underscoring that conviction was the Cuban Revolution that took place in the late 1950s and early 1960s. Refugees relocated throughout the eastern United States. Several refugee families came to Columbus, including one young boy who became part of my class in elementary school. Many were from the upper echelons of Cuban society. They came to the United States, our mother reminded us, "with nothing but the shirt on their back." That made a big impression on her and, consequently, on us. The conclusion our mother drew from their experience was "your education you can always take with you, and no one can take that away."

She made motherhood her vocational priority and drilled the importance of education into my brothers and sister and me. Among the gifts our mother gave us were the long hours she spent with each of us on our college admissions and scholarship applications. That touched us all deeply. She was dedicated to the proposition that education would make all the difference in our lives—which it did. And she practiced what she preached. As an avid library patron, she brought home and read stacks of books throughout her life. Her gift of intellectual curiosity stimulated her genuine interest in all the people whom she met.

Literally to the end of her life on November 16, 2009, our mother also was a proponent of the power of positive thinking. In one of her final moments of lucidity, after a prolonged struggle with Crohn's disease, I asked how she had managed to cope with so many years of adverse health. She reminded me to "always think positively; otherwise, you will not enjoy life."

In any event, thanks to the administrator's intervention, Marian enrolled in and graduated from Washington High School in the spring of 1943. World War II was a central fact of life for her and her classmates. The commencement address by Dr. Arthur J. Klein posed the question "Shall the schools be a wartime casualty?" The 1943 *Sunburst* yearbook noted, "The inevitable has happened. War has cast its devastating shadow on this land we love." The editors proclaimed that "no sacrifice is too great to assure the safety of those things which a freedom-loving people hold most precious. Undaunted," they avowed, "we have even offered human lives, for blood is not too great a price to pay for the countless blessings it has brought. Thus it is, with a fervent prayer," they solemnly wrote, "that we dedicate this book to the fighting men everywhere, spilling out their blood upon the altar of human sacrifice in order 'to secure the blessings of liberty for ourselves and our posterity.'"

The following year, Marian enrolled in Ohio University, starting with the fall semester of 1944 and continuing into the spring semester of 1945. After a one-year break, during which she worked in Cincinnati, she enrolled in the University of Cincinnati Evening College for business studies while also working for the university as a clerk-typist. She spent two semesters there and then returned to Ohio University in the fall semester of 1947, with a focus on studying to become a teacher. She also was a member of the Omega Nu Tau sorority. She attended Ohio University until January 1949, going from there into the working world, with a college degree remaining as an aspiration.

She then worked in a series of jobs, starting at Western Electric Company in Indianapolis with responsibility for filing engineering drawings, then moved to the William H. Block Company in Indianapolis, where she worked as secretary for an interior decorator. She applied successfully for a civil service position as a clerk-typist with the US Department of the Army at Fort Benjamin Harrison in Indianapolis and was promoted to a civil service stenographer position in January 1952, working as secretary to the post adjutant.

Meanwhile, Stanley also moved to Indianapolis after his college graduation and found a temporary room at the YMCA. He, too, worked early in his career through a series of jobs, including stints with International Harvester, with Universal CIT Corporation, with Quality Swift Homes, and as a self-employed contractor. On November 29, 1954, eight months after I was born, he started as an agent for Prudential Insurance Company, a position he held until his retirement just over thirty-one years later. His first post was in Cambridge, Ohio. An opportunity then arose to serve as a Prudential agent in Central Ohio.

My father and mother moved with me at that time to Grandview Heights, a Columbus suburb, into a two-story duplex, where we lived for almost four years. In the summer I could look out my bedroom window and see the "big boys" (who must only have been nine or ten years old) playing baseball in nearby Oxley Field (now known as Pierce Field) under the lights at night. Among my other distinctive memories of Grandview Heights are going out on Halloween night and riding the bus with my mother to the local public library, from which she and I each would borrow what seemed like armloads of books.

My Childhood

In 1959, when I was five, we moved into our new home in a new subdivision on the north side of Columbus. My brother Thomas had been born a few months before. For several months, on Sundays after church, we went with our parents to look at homes; they needed more room and permanence than our rented duplex in Grandview Heights had for their growing family. It was important to them to find a brick home with a workable floor plan and at least three bedrooms. They found what they were looking for at 1089 Fordham Road in the new neighborhood of Maize Meadows. The house and lot cost $19,000. Among the novelties of the three-bedroom home (for us) were a laundry chute and two bathrooms, including one with a sliding door. Perhaps reminiscent of the outside entryway into the cellar of my grandparents' home in Martins Ferry, one custom feature my father asked the builders to add was an outside entryway into the basement.

In an eerie confluence of events, it was the outside entryway through which the Columbus Fire and EMT team and I gained access to the locked house on the day in May 2010, six months after our mother died, when my brother Stanley called to say he was concerned because he had not been able to reach our dad for the past day or so. We found Dad in a living room chair, still alive but unconscious from a cerebral hemorrhage and stroke. After a brief but unavailing hospitalization, he died the next day. When I now think of the outside entryway, I cannot help but wonder if some subconscious forethought was responsible for its addition to our home.

We moved in on July 3, 1959, and we could see from our new backyard the fireworks display that evening from the Columbus Park of Roses several miles away on our new side of town. My other vivid memory of moving day is carrying in my small rocking chair, which remains in our family; our son Adam brought it into the new home into which he, Maryline, and I moved shortly before his sister Abigail was born. While it awaits its next move, the chair is now upstairs in our home in a spare bedroom filled with other family memorabilia.

Through the years of my childhood, the furnishings were modest, and our lifestyle was thrifty. Our parents kept plastic slipcovers on the couch and chairs in the living room to preserve them. Our mother made dinner almost every night (often cube steaks, hot dogs, or ham/Spam with vegetables), and our father occasionally grilled hot dogs and hamburgers on the barbeque. Sometimes, for a treat, we would order pizza. Every Christmas our mother went out of her way to bake her own array of traditional cookies, the best of which were her gingerbread men. For our first Christmas in our new home, our mother and father bought a live Christmas tree, which they planted afterward in the front yard on our treeless new street, and which ultimately grew to tower over the home.

Our new home was on the edge of town at the time. The main thoroughfare, Morse Road, just north of us, was still a two-lane country road with open fields on either side. (It is now a major arterial street with commercial development on both sides for several miles.) The residential streets in our subdivision were new, and homes were still being built on our road and other nearby streets when we moved in and for several years afterward. That scenario created a mindset beyond what I realized at the time. When you are raised in a growing part of town with new homes going up all around you, schools being built, businesses opening, and roads coming in, it is exciting. It was a positive environment in which to spend the early years of my life.

Amid the growth, a few abandoned farm homes along the existing roads that led to our neighborhood awaited their inevitable replacement by modern housing. They held treasures of their own for my adventure-seeking childhood friends and me. We were excited one day to find in one a stack of newspapers, carefully saved from 1945, with headlines announcing the end of World War II.

One big event was the construction of the new interstate highway that came through our part of town shortly after my family moved there. My father took me to see it one sunny, cold winter day. He parked the car, and we climbed up a hill on which the nearly finished freeway (now Interstate 71, at the Morse Road exit) spread before us in both directions. The new expressway was a major innovation, part of the National Defense Highway System created in June 1956 when President Dwight D. Eisenhower signed the authorizing legislation. That futuristic sight, amazing to me, seemed to open limitless horizons. For us as a practical matter, its completion would mean there would be no traffic lights or other stops between Columbus and family visits to Martins Ferry and Cincinnati.

Also novel was the construction of a modern shopping mall, one of the first of its kind locally, about a mile east of our home. The semi-enclosed Northland Mall included two big anchor stores (Lazarus and Sears) and a large collection of other retailers. Its opening was heralded as a wave of the future.

It was impossible to grow up in such an age and place and not sense there were endless possibilities. All around us, everything was growing, everything was booming, everything was moving. In the sky above us, the Space Race was underway. I remember scanning the night skies for glimpses of what might be the Russian satellite Sputnik orbiting overhead and waking up with a sense of wonder on the mornings when the three television networks, broadcasting live from Cape Canaveral, Florida, awaited the launches of a series of manned American spacecraft in the Mercury, Gemini, and Apollo space programs. The television presentation of the launches was dramatic, even though it was just in black and white. The networks preempted their regular programming to air the countdowns and takeoffs. We learned about the astronauts and their missions and the progress our nation was making as the spacecraft went farther and farther into space—on the way to the moon. You could feel the tide of history flowing positively forward.

It was a stable and modest middle-class neighborhood, full of young families with busy lives. There were mostly single-family homes, with apartment buildings on the periphery. Our neighbors worked in a variety of jobs. There was an administrator at the Ohio High School Athletic Association, a young dentist, an associate professor, an employee of the Metropolitan Park District, a systems and procedures specialist at the US Defense Construction Supply Center, a claims director at the Ohio Bureau of Workers' Compensation, an insurance agent, an officer of the American Contract Bridge League, and employees of other companies and agencies, with various occupations.

As was then the norm, it was usually the husband and father who worked at such jobs while the wife and mother maintained the home and handled family responsibilities. At-home entertainment in the evenings and on weekends included riding our bicycles, playing hide-and-seek and card games, and watching vacation pictures as a slideshow or on a reel-to-reel movie projector.

I got to know the area and all the neighbors well, as I had a newspaper route. I delivered *The Columbus Dispatch* in the afternoons and on Sunday mornings for three and a half years, from Christmas Eve 1967 to June 1971. Every Thursday night after supper, I would go back out and collect the weekly payment, retracing my door-to-door delivery route. The full-week subscription was sixty-seven cents (seven cents for the six daily newspapers and twenty-five cents for the Sunday edition). If I was lucky, the customer would give me seventy-five cents and say, "Keep the change," which was a huge tip at the time.

My father, brothers Stanley and Tom, mother, sister Susan, and I prepare a daily edition of The Columbus Dispatch *for delivery on the newspaper route I had carried and my brothers continued. (Reproduced with permission from © Fred Shannon – USA TODAY NETWORK via Imagn Images.)*

Summarizing "what the newspaper route has meant to me" at age sixteen, after three years of service, I wrote to the Selection Committee for the Glenn L. Cox Scholarship Award that "at first the route had a great material value to me. There were opportunities to make money, win prizes, and take interesting trips. But soon the route began to mean more to me than many material things. The paper route has taught me the value and rewards of work. I've learned how to handle money and, more importantly, how to organize my time. . . . Through the money earned on the paper route, I've become partially self-supporting. This is a help to my parents. The money I've earned has given me funds with which to pay my tuition [at St. Francis de Sales High School, which I recall being $250 per semester] and buy other school materials, as well as my clothing; and also to start a savings account for college." The savings account amounted to $866 at the time.

One other key point about *The Columbus Dispatch* newspaper route was that "although I've had eleven years of formal education, the people I've worked with on my route have added much to my knowledge by experience which I could not have obtained from books. Through the route, I've come in contact with many different types of people and personalities from all walks of life and many professions. The experiences I have had with my customers have taught me much about human nature, and this will certainly be helpful in the future, as it is right now."

In a forecast of things to come, I observed that "my contact with people every day, especially on the paper route, has influenced me to go into politics and the study of law. I'm interested in these subjects because I love what we've got here in the United States. Although we're sailing through some pretty rough seas right now [in 1970, as the divisive Vietnam War and changing cultural norms roiled American life], America will survive because she is founded on principles and ideals sacred to men everywhere. One of the most revered of our 'inalienable rights' is the Freedom of the Press. I hope that I have, by delivering the newspapers to the people, contributed toward keeping the beacon of freedom shining in America. This is one way of helping our country, one way in which I feel I can be effective as a teenager."

The route grew from 78 customers at the beginning to 125 at the end. With the help of letters of recommendation from newspaper customers, teachers, and school administrators, I was fortunate to win the Outstanding Newspaperboy 1971 award from *The Columbus Dispatch*. My brothers took over the route in June 1971, when I left for a summer program on the campus of The Ohio State University. They added several more years of timely (and dry) newspaper delivery to our neighborhood.

Along with several classmates, I supplemented the income from the newspaper route by selling refreshments at Ohio State home football games for two seasons, starting in the fall of 1968. It was an exciting time to be in Ohio Stadium, as the Buckeyes, under Coach Woody Hayes, took many fans by surprise in the 1968 season, securing a national title—undefeated—as a team many now consider to have been one of the strongest in the history of the OSU football program. While ecstatic fans celebrated all around us on a succession of dramatic Saturday afternoons, my buddies and I walked up and down the aisles of each deck, peddling Coca-Cola ("Coke, here. Ice-cold Coke here. Get your ice-cold Coke here.") we bought by the trayful at a wholesale price and sold on a retail basis. It was a lucrative job. Less sensationally but still helpful as a source of income, I also cut grass for many neighbors during the summers, shoveled snow in the winters, and worked for several months as a dishwasher at a nearby restaurant.

The Cub Scouts and Boy Scouts were a big part of my life. In addition to weekly meetings, service activities, and merit badge programs, we went on many campouts in wilderness areas and Scout camps around Ohio. We would pitch tents and sleep in sleeping bags, build campfires, cook our own meals, go hiking and canoeing, whittle wood, and take part in other outdoor activities. The overriding rule was to leave the area better than we had found it. Our fathers taught us many of the necessary skills based on what they had learned in the military during World War II or the Korean War. Most of my friends at the time were other boys in the Scouting program.

Swimming also became a part of my life in those years. Our family occasionally bought passes to one of the two outdoor pools (Sequoia Pool and Northland Pool) several blocks from our home. I took swimming lessons and went to those pools in the afternoons or evenings when time allowed. For a few summers, I got to go for a full week to Camp St. Joseph, run by the Catholic Diocese of Columbus, which also had an outdoor pool in which I enjoyed swimming. Little did I know at the time what a big difference swimming would make in my life many years later.

The Bedrock of a Stable Family

Because of our age differences, my brothers and sister and I were doing different things at the same time at home and school but shared the family experience. We still spend many holidays together. We are lucky to have developed a relationship when we were younger that we have been able to sustain beyond childhood. That came largely from being subject to the same expectations of our parents at home and at school, especially in terms of education and personal habits.

Those expectations led my brother Tom to earn a bachelor of fine arts from the Columbus College of Art and Design. He has had a brilliant creative streak; he was an Eagle Scout, and as a lifeguard and water safety instructor, he rescued four swimmers from drowning. He now works for St. Mary's School and, with his wife Michelle, an educator, lives in Columbus. My brother Stanley earned his undergraduate degree cum laude from Miami University and a master's degree and PhD from Vanderbilt University, and he has become a child psychologist in Washington, DC. My sister Susan graduated cum laude from Capital University with a bachelor of science in nursing and from The Ohio State University with a master's degree as a pediatric nurse practitioner. She has worked as a pediatric intensive care nurse at several top-ranked children's hospitals and is now a nursing instructor. Susan and her husband John, a lawyer, live in Gurnee, Illinois, north of Chicago, and have two highly accomplished and winsome children, Elizabeth and Nicholas.

Family trips in the summers strengthened our childhood bonds. As an agent for Prudential Insurance, my father benefitted from the company's incentive awards program that enabled agents to go to a convention if they sold a certain amount of insurance coverage. He qualified several times. The drives to the convention destinations usually stretched out over several days. On the way, we stayed at Howard Johnson's motels or other such places. Our route was set out in a AAA TripTik, which was a spiral-bound tablet-type compilation of road maps provided by the American Automobile Association. It detailed the route to take and suggested places to visit and stay. When we stayed in motels that had outdoor pools, it was a real treat. We took an ice chest filled with sandwiches, soft drinks, and water for lunch along the way at roadside rest areas. My father was the only driver, so he had his work cut out for him.

In 1965, for example, we went to the World's Fair in New York. For a young boy from the Midwest, the city was astonishing. What made the biggest impression was the scale of things—how big the city was in comparison to Columbus, how big the buildings were, how many people filled the streets, the noise, and the constant activity, day and night. We stayed in a huge hotel in midtown Manhattan. The World's Fair was exciting because most of the major nations had pavilions there, so visitors could learn a little bit about each one. The fair was in Queens, New York. I did not have a sense of what the different boroughs were but had heard scary stories about life in the big city. As it turned out, everything was fine, and we had a fantastic trip that substantially broadened my horizons.

The convention trip to Colorado had a similar effect on my imagination. Along the way we stopped in St. Louis, then visited the museums for Presidents Harry S. Truman (in Independence, Missouri) and Dwight D. Eisenhower (in Abilene, Kansas). I was interested in history and politics, so those places were fascinating. At the Air Force Academy in Colorado Springs, I committed to memory the reminder on the base of a winged statue that "man's flight through life is sustained by the power of his knowledge." A visit to the top of Pike's Peak was a highlight of the vacation. The Colorado trip was also distinguished by the fact that we had quite a full car. It was a new white Chevrolet Impala with a red interior, to which my father added an air-conditioning unit (our first). The car held seven of us: my mother (five months pregnant with our sister Susan), my father, Tom, Stanley, Grandma Kulewicz, my cousin Matt, and me.

The conventions accounted for most, but not all, of our family vacations. A family sightseeing trip to Washington, DC, was exciting. My parents had been there on their honeymoon. For us children, it was the first time we saw and were inspired by the Capitol, the Lincoln Memorial, the Washington Monument, the White House, the Bureau of Engraving and Printing, and other prominent landmarks.

I had cousins with whom I also shared many youthful experiences and adventures on occasional weekends and in the summers. The Ottos lived in Martins Ferry. With five children, my Aunt Stella ran a tight ship at home. She engaged herself fully in whatever she was doing and always spoke and acted in a direct and forthright way. She was loved by her family and respected by the people of Martins Ferry, who elected her later in life to serve five terms on the city council. Uncle Lewis was a no-nonsense man who seemed larger than life to me because of his physical strength, his service in the US Navy during World War II in the Pacific Theater on an LST-811 boat, and the tattoos on his forearms. He worked at the Yorkville plant of Wheeling Steel and, on his own, built the home in which he and Aunt Stella raised their family.

Cousin Janet was a bright child who paved the way to college for her family at Ohio University, where she earned a bachelor of science in biology and a master's degree in elementary school counseling. She loved intellectual challenges and never failed to think for herself. Janet merged her passions for science and education by becoming an elementary school counselor. Devoted to improving the lives of children from all backgrounds, she worked in schools in Ohio and Michigan and served as a Girl Scout troop leader. It was a sad day for our entire family when Janet passed away at age forty-two from Hodgkin's disease, leaving behind her husband Michael McEvoy and their daughter Erin.

My cousin Matthew worked at the Martins Ferry and Yorkville plants of Wheeling-Pittsburgh Steel in production and as a crane operator and electrician and served as treasurer and a trustee of the United Steelworkers local. During strikes and occasional layoffs, and after closure of the mills, he worked as an IBEW wireman and as an instrumentation and electrical technician for other employers. Matt has remained in the Ohio Valley with his wife Anna, their son Joseph, and their daughter Alyssa.

My cousin Joe's first job was in an underground coal mine, where he worked for four years and was a member of the United Mine Workers Union. His fellow miners, whom he admired as men who "worked hard, took care of their families and looked out for their friends, neighbors and co-workers," urged him to get out of the mine and go back to college. He ultimately earned an electrical engineering degree. His career trajectory changed dramatically when a start-up company recruited him to work in the robotic applications sector, which led to his immersion in several major technology disruptions of the past four decades. He and his wife Marti raised three daughters (Jenny, Katie, and Marissa) and live in the Cincinnati area.

My cousin Andy worked for two years after high school in a coal mine as a shuttle car operator and inside safety inspector. He then got degrees in electrical engineering technology and business before beginning a successful forty-year career with Xerox, based in Columbus. Andy and his wife Sherl have three children (Stephanie, Michael, and Andrea) and live in the Columbus area.

Cousin Nancy received a nursing degree from Ohio State and worked in neonatal and cardiac intensive care. With her husband Kevin, a successful biotech entrepreneur who graduated from OSU with a bachelor of science in mechanical engineering and from Ohio University with an MBA, she raised their children (Angela and Stephen) in Delaware and Massachusetts.

My cousin Mike lived in rural southwest Ohio near the town of Okeana. He was sufficiently older than me (three-plus years) that I looked up to him a lot when we were kids and loved the life he was living out in the country. Our Grandpa Tuggle took over some of the parenting responsibilities after Mike's mother lost her life in a December 1963 car crash. Mike married when he was twenty-one and served during the Vietnam era in the US Marines. He was stationed in Okinawa when he was in a fatal motorcycle accident a few days before I finished law school. His daughter Michelle now lives in Ohio.

For my brothers and sister and me, the most poignant moments were the days our parents died. Our mother passed away in November 2009, and our father died six months later, in May 2010. Our mother was successful in keeping our focus on school and educational opportunities. Writing about our dad in a Father's Day article that highlighted our newspaper route, a *Columbus Dispatch* reporter observed he "said he doesn't like to push his children. Rather, he tries to counsel them and live as a good example for them to follow." Like our mother with education, he, too, was successful in what he had sought to do as a parent. Together, they lived a richly rewarding life, having set out in the post-war years to get married, buy a home, and raise a family. They went through the usual hardships and frustrations of raising a family. When each of them died, though, their family was gathered lovingly around them—truly successful lives and a genuine blessing by the most important worldly measure of all.

Chapter 2:
School Years

The years in elementary and secondary school gave me many opportunities I did not fully appreciate until later in life. I started kindergarten in 1959, in a half-day program at Northridge School, a public school on the north side of Columbus. My teacher was Roberta M. Sunbury, a kind lady whose encouragement with the alphabet and reading got my formal education off to a positive start.

Starting Out: St. Matthias Elementary School

I went to grade school at St. Matthias Elementary School, a neighborhood parochial school on the north side of Columbus that is still in existence today. As part of an expansion parish of the diocese at the time, the school was newly constructed and consisted mainly of classrooms, a gymnasium space, and a small administrative office. The development of the community was happening at such a rapid pace and resources apparently were so limited there was no time to build a separate church, so the gymnasium served as the improvised location of the parish church for all the years I was there.

Going to parochial school gives the student a sense of mission, which I took for granted at the time but came to better understand as I grew older. For a few years in grade school, my ambition was to become a priest. I was drawn to the splendor and mystery of the Roman Catholic Church. Until third or fourth grade, when the goal of becoming a lawyer displaced it, I assumed it would be my calling.

Things got off to a smooth start scholastically with a good first-grade teacher, Mrs. Schirtzinger. I enjoyed going to school and loved the learning process. The teaching style was something I was able to connect with. (Nowadays, schools have adopted a variety of teaching methods designed to connect with many different learning styles. I frequently wonder how much more beneficial that would have been for many of my classmates whom the standard teaching process of that era was not able to effectively reach.) My parents were excited when I came home one day early in the school year with a holy card, for having correctly (according to the Baltimore Catechism of the Catholic Church) answered the question "Why did God make me?" with the response "To know, love, and serve God."

The classrooms at St. Matthias quickly filled to the brim. In second grade, there were fifty-two of us in one classroom alone—with just one nun to teach us. Her religious name was Sister Dominic Savio; she is now Sister Barbara Gilmetti. Given the sheer number of students in the classroom, she necessarily was scrupulous in making sure we all behaved and remained focused. I had the good fortune of visiting Sister Barbara a few years ago at a residence in Massachusetts for members of the Sisters of Charity of Nazareth, the order to which she has belonged for over sixty-eight years now. She is still teaching, in a career that has ranged from elementary schools around the nation to tutorial work with underprivileged children in Mississippi and four summers with the Sioux Tribe in South Dakota. Her first cousin was a Carmelite priest, Father Louis V. Scagnelli, who encouraged my interest in a priestly vocation by giving me a small model of an altar, which I still have.

I was just as fortunate in the rest of the elementary school grades. My teachers were Miss Joseph in third grade, Mrs. Hollern in fourth grade, Mrs. Bidstrup in fifth grade, Miss Serafin (later Mrs. Yager) in sixth and seventh grades, and Sister Charles Augustine (later Sister Elizabeth Ball) in eighth grade. They each were understanding and thoughtful educators who dedicated themselves to my classmates and me. Seeing now the positive difference they made in my growth, I wish it were possible to thank them personally and let them know how much I appreciate and respect them.

In seventh grade, we had a history teacher named Dan Massey. He was twenty-three years old and was a night law school student. He had a dashing aura and would come to school dressed in three-piece suits and driving a Corvette, which made him seem like the coolest guy in the world. I loved history and knew by then I wanted to go to law school, so he became a role model for me. More than he likely realized, but as I have subsequently been able to tell him, he made a big impression on me. Hoping, in turn, to impress him, I drummed up confidence to call the law school dean at Ohio State to interview him for a paper I was writing about the *Dred Scott* decision of 1857. Mr. Massey turned eighty recently and still lives in Columbus, where he remains active in the state government as a member of the Ohio Industrial Commission.

In my spare time, when I was not playing outside in the neighborhood, I read a lot of books. The first was *The Day Lincoln Was Shot* by Jim Bishop. I must have been in second or third grade and found it when I was staying with Grandma and Grandpa Tuggle in their trailer in Indianapolis. I started reading and was completely absorbed. I knew who Abraham Lincoln was and that he had been a lawyer, but I did not know he had been assassinated. It was in a volume of the Reader's Digest Condensed Books. Grandpa Tuggle saw I was so excited to read the book that he let me keep it—a volume I still have. I started to learn more about the Civil War from all I was reading, and my love of American history continued to grow.

Other books included biographies and American history stories. My parents subscribed to *Reader's Digest* and *Time* magazine, which I became accustomed to reading. I also recall reading *The Power of Positive Thinking* by Dr. Norman Vincent Peale and finding a lot to like in the point he made about how positivity can change our lives for the better. Other prized reading material came from my mother's aunt, Marie Coumar, who lived just outside New York City. When sending us gifts at Christmas, she would sometimes enclose them in pages of *The New York Times*, which I was as excited to receive as the presents themselves.

As we were made aware in school, the Roman Catholic Church was undergoing a major reform at the time, in the course of the Vatican II Ecumenical Council of 1962–1965. The change manifested itself in the language of the Mass, which switched from the traditional Latin to English in the United States (shortly after I had become an altar boy trained in the Latin rite), the reconfiguration of churches to turn the altars around and have the priest facing the congregation, the adoption of a more open and tolerant relationship with other religions and denominations, the seeming relaxation of certain rules, and other changes meant to connote a modernization of the Church. The Sisters of Charity of Nazareth who taught us at St. Matthias changed their names from the adopted names of saints to their own given names. The Vatican II Council seemed to add momentum to the changes going on all around us.

In a fainter tone, we also began to hear about a scientific advance my contemporaries and I did not fully understand at the time but that would come to be regarded by some as the most revolutionary development of the twentieth century—the birth control pill. Its gradual spread would soon confront the Church and its members with major doctrinal unease. It would completely upend established assumptions and practices throughout society about gender equality, sexual activity, and family planning. The traditional template of early marriage, employed fathers and stay-at-home mothers, was about to shift in a big way.

Widespread societal acceptance of the new birth control pill and other forms of contraception would ultimately mean that my contemporaries and I would come of age and live as adults in a world very different—in terms of family structures, job opportunities, sexual conduct, and gender equality— than the seemingly conventional one into which we had been born. We each would have to find our own way as the world around us totally changed.

In politics as well, the nation was changing. One clear memory from my early days in grade school is of the morning after John F. Kennedy was elected president in 1960. I was in first grade—six years old. I stayed up on election night, watching the television as the election returns came in. It was the first time I had been aware of an election. I knew who then-Senator Kennedy was and that he was Catholic. The outcome was not decided by the time I went to bed, but the next day, late in the morning, someone came down the hall, knocking on the classroom doors and joyfully shouting, "He won, he won!"

In fourth grade, as a sad counterpoint, was the tragic day President Kennedy died. We learned first that he had been shot in Dallas and taken to a hospital; then, we waited for further news in our classroom, which was provisionally located in the high school next to St. Matthias. About an hour later, the high school principal, Father James M. Berendt, came onto the public address system and solemnly asked each teacher to "please lead your students in saying the Rosary for the repose of the soul of President Kennedy." We all left school quietly at the end of the day, shocked and mournful along with the rest of the nation.

President Kennedy inspired people of all generations in the United States. One personal impact upon me was to spark what would become a lifelong interest in government and the political process. My first foray into politics as a candidate was in sixth grade when I ran (unsuccessfully) for class president. With the benefit of my parents' consolation and advice, I was able to absorb a lot of lessons from what felt like a devastating defeat and managed to succeed in the class president elections in seventh and eighth grade.

In that capacity, my seventh-grade teacher thought I "conducted extremely worthwhile class meetings. These included vigorous and intelligent discussions on current problems, such as school spirit, racial issues, political controversies, and other varied topics. Every member of the class eventually participated in discussions and activities under John's directions." Balancing her praise, she also noted I sometimes "played unoffensive pranks."

I do not recall the specific pranks, but I did engage in my share of youthful misadventures outside the classroom. None of the mischief seemed grave or unusual, especially in the context of my life at the time, but in retrospect, I was lucky to have avoided any adverse consequences.

Throughout the 1960s, the civil rights movement was flourishing in a way that was inspirational to me. I vividly remember the March on Washington, which took place on August 28, 1963. It was a hot and humid summer afternoon, in Washington and at home. The television was on in our living room, with the drapes drawn and doors open. With no air conditioning, one small fan gave us some relief from the heat. The march was exciting to watch. To me, it seemed to show the trajectory of the nation unfolding in what I felt was a positive direction. It gave me great hope, inspiration, and confidence that it was a wonderful time to be alive.

I became aware of the civil rights movement from the news on television and conversations of grown-ups in the course of their daily activities. It was obviously a big challenge to the status quo, and people often talked about it. It was stirring—and unsettling. Racial discrimination was so plainly wrong, but people were not seeing eye to eye. Among other breakthrough moments, from my own perspective, was the Sunday morning when one of the priests at St. Matthias Church took the initiative to address racial equality in his homily. It was wrong to discriminate against people on the basis of their race, he simply said, and essential to remember that Black people pay the same taxes, are called upon to make the same sacrifices in the same military, and worship the same God as white people. It was the only occasion on which our all-white parish had heard such a message at Mass, which gave even more weight to the occasion.

People of Polish descent had to contend with a different form of prejudice in the United States during those years, as Polish "jokes" proliferated. As Poles came to America in the early twentieth century, most jobs available to them involved only physical labor, subjecting the immigrants to ethnic-based derision. The point of the "jokes" was to stereotype and demean the intelligence and ability of people with Polish ancestry. The so-called humor was disparaging and offensive, unconsciously echoing the Nazi stereotyping of Poles as subhuman. It was hardly ever condemned, even as Poles moved into the middle class. But adversity strengthened us. For the most part, it served only to steel the resolve of Polish Americans to show those who indulged in such ridicule how misinformed they were.

My parents only occasionally talked about politics and social matters, but they were mindful of the environment in which we lived. I started to express political interest when I was quite young. My mother and father were respectful of government but skeptical about politics, and they feared I would go straight into politics without any other experience or profession. They were not especially happy about that. They thought it was more important to first get a college education and go to law school and then maybe go into politics.

So many of the political issues then were like today's problems. Inflation, crime, the Middle East, and other such topics have proved to be perennial matters of national discourse. Racial discrimination issues were as pressing then as they are now. We came across segregation practices on a family road trip to Florida in the early 1960s. I was old enough to read and, in a south Georgia restaurant, saw a line at the bottom of the menu that said "We reserve the right to refuse service to any individual." That puzzled me. I asked my father a little too loudly what it meant. He explained in a hushed voice it meant the restaurant could refuse to serve nonwhite customers. I was aware of growing up in a predominantly white environment in our neighborhood and at school, but such outright discrimination as the restaurant "reserved the right" to practice seemed shameful.

Culturally, the early 1964 arrival of the Beatles in the United States felt like a turning point. I watched one of their television debuts on *The Ed Sullivan Show*. It was a historic event and seemed to offer a new, fresh view of the world. In November 1963, with the assassination of President Kennedy, the nation lost a young leader who embodied the spirit of the times. His successor, President Lyndon B. Johnson, had enormous legislative clout but a far different sort of popular appeal. The change that the election of President Kennedy had ushered in seemed, to me, to be interrupted. But the arrival of the Beatles a few months afterward was like a generational shift in popular culture.

Popular culture was undergoing a major change around all of us in my school and neighborhood. The change became widely accessible with the spread of transistor radios. The now-obsolete handheld radios, about the size of our current smartphones, allowed us to listen to stations that played the new music we liked. Our parents sometimes discouraged us from listening. Our teachers certainly did. At school we had been forbidden to listen to a song by Tommy James and the Shondells called "I Think We're Alone Now," which the faculty direly warned would give us "impure thoughts." That explanation naturally aroused our curiosity and made it all the more exciting to listen to the song whenever the radio stations played it.

The world changed greatly in the course of my eight years in elementary school. The postwar conformity of the 1950s gave way to what would become a new age that defied cultural norms. As a high school and college student, I would sometimes find myself responding to the new norms and freedoms in ways that, to this day, leave me questioning my maturity at the time.

Growing Up and Moving On: St. Francis de Sales High School

Having graduated from St. Matthias Elementary School in June 1968, I moved in the fall across the parking lot to St. Francis de Sales High School. It was the newest parochial high school in the community, having opened in the early 1960s, so I was in one of the first classes there. The school put a lot of emphasis on discipline, starting with uniforms; boys had to wear a dress shirt and tie, while girls wore a prescribed jumper and blouse. The faculty particularly rewarded effort and academic achievement. The occasional "late-nighters" in elementary school became more frequent in high school as I dealt with more homework and school projects.

I understood that secondary school was one step in the process— that I was likely to go to college and, even at that age, I hoped to go to law school. I got a good, broad education and was fortunate enough to do well academically. Along the way I also was a member of the Key Club (affiliated with the Kiwanis Club service organization) and National Honor Society, and I was the assistant editor of our school newspaper.

Like most other schools, De Sales had a student council. With an abiding interest in government and politics stoked by President Kennedy and others, I moved up through the various roles. I served as secretary-treasurer and vice president of the student council, and then as president of the senior class. It was an ongoing learning experience. With a class of 210 people, running for election in such a microcosm shed light on how the same process operated on a far larger scale. Among the lessons I learned was the importance of actually asking everyone for their vote. No one should ever be taken for granted. The campaign slogan "Keep cool with Kulewicz" proved to be a winning one. The school also indulged my political interests by allowing me to organize an evening debate on the premises between representatives of the two candidates for governor of Ohio (John Gilligan and Roger Cloud) in the fall of 1970.

I took to heart wise advice I received later that fall from US Senator Edmund S. Muskie of Maine. He had come to national attention two years earlier, as the 1968 vice-presidential nominee for the Democratic Party. His Polish ancestry caused me to hold him in high esteem. I wrote to him during the summer of 1970, asking how he had gotten into politics and how one could be successful at it. He wrote back in November.

He recounted his early political career. "It wasn't easy in those days," he wrote, "being a Democrat in a Republican-controlled state. The Republicans were, in a sense, the establishment. I had to learn the skills of persuasion and I bucked the establishment in running for governor in 1954. And I won." He attributed his success to the fact that he had "always believed in spelling out the issues candidly to the people and not engaging in a lot of rhetoric or name-calling." He took pride in having brought into the Maine Democratic Party and legislature a new generation "with ideas about saving what needs to be saved while moving forward economically and we have done it by talking sense to the people."

Senator Muskie's advice was that "you have the right instincts. The best thing to do now is study hard and yet don't forget about talking with people and learning what they care about and what they need." His letter was a real treasure to me and remains a prized possession.

Some of my friends and classmates thought my interest in politics was peculiar, but I saw it as part of becoming a lawyer and getting involved in public affairs. The Vietnam War took center stage in 1968, which was a particularly tumultuous year. Martin Luther King Jr. and Robert F.

Kennedy were shot, the Democratic National Convention culminated in an immense upheaval within the party, and Richard M. Nixon was elected president. Following those events were the Woodstock festival in 1969 and the shootings at Kent State University in Ohio the next year, when four protesting students were slain in a fusillade by the Ohio National Guard. It gave us much to consider, particularly as the fatalities at Kent State had occurred so close to home. It all seemed like such a complicated contrast to the simple moral and political clarity of the World War II generation. It was an environment in which one could easily become confused or strident.

Guided by Senator Muskie's advice, I continued to concentrate on my studies. My high school teachers encouraged me academically, some in creative ways. Chemistry was one area in which I struggled. I just could not understand the subject. I could read the book and do my homework long into the night, but it would not sink in. I was having a difficult time. Mr. John Duffy was the chemistry teacher. Like Mr. Massey when I was in grade school, he was also studying at night school to become a lawyer. He could see I needed help—and that my lack of understanding was not from a lack of effort. This was in 1970, the year after the moon landing on July 20, 1969, by members of the Apollo 11 crew. We were having a science fair. I wanted to do a project on the Apollo 11 mission. Mr. Duffy said, "I'll make you a deal. If you can get moon rocks to go with it here to the high school for the science fair, I'll give you an A in chemistry."

It was a challenge I was happy to accept. "Nothing's impossible if you put your mind to it," as I told a newspaper interviewer. "That's what interested me in Apollo 11. It was achieving the impossible dream." The first man to walk on the moon, Neil A. Armstrong, was from Wapakoneta, Ohio. I had gone with my parents to see his hometown—and with a friend and his mother to attend the homecoming parade after Armstrong's return from the moon. I knew the National Aeronautics and Space Administration had sent several moon rock samples to the Ohio Historical Society.

I managed to find the right person to contact and was able to convince the historical society to bring the moon rocks to the high school for the science fair. *The Catholic Times* reported that "the De Sales science fair marked the first appearance [of the moon rock samples] in a high school" and that they "were taken to and from the school in an armored car." Our principal, Father Berendt, joked at the school assembly for the moon rocks presentation that "John's invited me to the White House when he becomes president in 2003." I had said no such thing but was tempted to reply that it was only because Father Berendt had invited me to the Vatican when he becomes pope. He was way too intimidating of a disciplinarian to take the risk of such a wisecrack, so I kept it to myself.

High school was not all scholastic work. Outside of academics, I was a member of the varsity track team, running mostly distance races. I was best at the 440-yard (quarter-mile) and 880-yard (half-mile) races. I did not come close to setting any records but was competitive, and I liked the training and being part of the team. My most memorable (to me) race was an 880 that I won because my mind was in the right place at the right time. Rather than dwelling on what I thought I was or was not capable of doing, I ran without any thought of limitations. Freed of self-consciousness, I took off and was able to maintain the faster pace. The win surprised everybody, including the coach. "Kulewicz, how did you do that?" he exclaimed. It was one of the first questions he had ever asked me, having noted on the contrary (with exasperation) early one season, "Kulewicz, you ask a lot of questions."

The Ohio Governor's School

A special break came my way in the summer of 1971, between junior and senior year. Earlier that year, I had applied for and was accepted into a new program called the Ohio Governor's School, modeled on the White House Fellows program. The curriculum consisted of a ten-week internship in state government that would "expose high school students and college freshmen directly to the problems of maintaining personal integrity while working within a bureaucracy." It was "believed to be the only program of its kind which elevates students in the seventeen- to nineteen-year age bracket . . . to actual participation in government." The program included twenty high school and college students from throughout Ohio. We lived in the Haverfield House dormitory at The Ohio State University and were assigned to various departments of the executive branch of the state government.

The application process included a self-assessment of strengths and weaknesses. I presumptuously wrote that "seventeen years of living have taught me that if a person is determined to do something, and if he puts his whole heart into it, he can succeed." After therefore listing "perseverance and determination" first in the strengths column, I listed "initiative" second, with the explanation that "too often we allow ourselves to be intimidated by what we believe to be impossible." I lauded myself also for my "ability to accept responsibility and lead a project until it is completed" and "a deeply rooted desire to find out about the world and its inhabitants." As for weaknesses, I quoted my English teacher, who had written to the newspaper award committee the year before that curiosity and ambition "often cause him to take on more work than he is able to handle because of the limitations of time" but also noted "he is still able to consistently produce good work." Occasional impatience and inability to express myself clearly were other weaknesses I acknowledged.

I advised the selection committee of my plan to go to college and law school and explained that "the research and study we will complete this summer on the problems of the State of Ohio will be a tremendous aid to me when I set out to help solve those problems" if successful at seeking elective office. "Personal action is the avenue to progress," I wrote, and "by learning what action is needed, I can begin my journey down that road."

The application was successful. In sending me off to live on the OSU campus that summer, my parents gave me a list of reminders, including the importance of table manners, thank-you notes, and the need to "obey the rules" and "get enough sleep." They urged me also to "keep your dorm room neat. You might have important visitors." My "visitors" were mostly the other students in the program, but the dormitory experience broadened my own horizons dramatically in exposing me to other people my age whose backgrounds were far different from my own. Having grown up in suburban Columbus and gone to local Catholic schools for virtually my entire life, it was one of my first chances to get to know students from rural Ohio and the inner cities, students who were Protestant and Jewish, and students who were from far wealthier families or more intellectual than me. It was a bigger adjustment than I would have thought—but one I am glad now to have had at an early age.

My internship placement was with the Ohio Department of Development under the auspices of Director David C. Sweet, a young and innovative leader who had earned a PhD and specialized in geography, economics, and planning. Dr. Sweet was characteristic of the bright young talent the 1970 election of John J. Gilligan as governor had infused into the state government. My primary assignment was to assist in preparation of a study called "Ohio 2000," which focused on objectives for business development in the state of Ohio leading up to the twenty-first century, then still nearly three decades away.

Firsthand exposure to politics added to the appeal of the Governor's School. Several high-ranking elected officials of both major political parties came to talk with us about issues with which they were dealing, including many reforms sought by the Gilligan administration, and public service more generally. The guests included the Speaker of the Ohio House of Representatives and several administration officials. We were invited to various political events, including the Ohio Democratic Party annual dinner. Having had an exciting time beforehand on an American Legion trip to Washington, DC, and at the American Legion's Buckey Boys State program at the beginning of the summer, I continued to nurture an interest in public service and told a local newspaper reporter covering the program that I wanted "to get people involved" in the political process.

The entire experience of living away from home and working for ten weeks in the upper echelons of the state government—especially at such a young age—was a windfall that gave me an unlimited opportunity to grow. It was a chance to work behind the scenes with high-ranking officials of the state government. That gave me a good glimpse of how complicated some issues and problems can be and how important it is for a leader to set clear priorities and understand people whose interests are at stake. I am amazed in retrospect at the patience of those to whom a naive teenager like me had been assigned for supervision and have been grateful ever since for what I learned from them.

Applying to The Ohio State University and Winning a Joyce Scholarship

As I progressed through high school, and especially after the Ohio Governor's School experience, there was no doubt in my mind that I would apply to college, and I very much wanted to go to The Ohio State University. It was the only college I was familiar with, and I enjoyed being in Ohio, so it seemed the obvious choice. I was aware of other colleges and universities around the nation, but nearly all of them seemed out of reach financially.

I applied for and was fortunate to win a Joyce Scholarship to Ohio State. The Glenna R. Joyce Scholarship paid the full tuition and room and board and provided a stipend for books and other educational expenses for (at the time) three students from Franklin County, where Columbus is located. The generosity of the four-year scholarship made an enormous difference in my college experience by not only defraying the cost but also making it possible to live in the dormitories. It also meant my parents did not need to worry about supporting me financially.

The process of applying for the scholarship was intense, under the supervision of my mother. It included writing an essay and having an interview. As I was interested in politics, the interviewers talked with me about the Electoral College—the body to which the United States Constitution gives the ultimate authority for selection of the president and vice president—and how it operates and why I was in favor of the process. They seemed surprised that a high school student would have that much interest in such an arcane subject and defend the Electoral College so staunchly. (Support on my part that has never wavered because the United States Constitution created a state-based federal government, which the

Electoral College accentuates.) Luckily, I was able to communicate well with them, and they awarded me one of the Joyce Scholarships to Ohio State that year.

My mother deserves much of the credit for the success of my scholarship application. Education was her number one priority for my brothers and sister and me. She was unrelenting in her attention to our completion of applications, composition of written essays, and compilation of the information that accompanied them. It was a stroke of good fortune to have a mother like her who really cared. If she had not been as insistent about putting together a top-notch application and getting it done on time—and supplementing it with all the necessary materials—I do not know how I would have managed the college admissions and scholarship process.

Chapter 3:
The Ohio State University

My college education began in September 1972 when I moved into a dormitory on the campus of The Ohio State University in Columbus and got underway with my undergraduate studies.

Studying American History

The four-year undergraduate curriculum at Ohio State required a lot of concentrated effort. I majored in history, with an emphasis on American history, and enrolled in as many classes as I could with several first-rate professors who were stellar educators; they were deeply engaged in what they were doing. They included Gary W. Reichard, with whom I studied extensively; Michael Les Benedict; R. Clayton Roberts Jr.; John Rothney; Warren Van Tine; and others. They were exceptionally devoted to their work as historians. Their classes included three consecutive courses on US history and courses on the history of the American labor movement, American political parties, American foreign policy, the Fourteenth Amendment, Tudor and Stuart England, and twentieth-century France. They each inspired not only excitement about the eras in which they specialized but also an appreciation of the importance of thoroughness, accuracy, and perspective. I still think of them and the lessons and habits they taught me about research, writing, and historical analysis.

I loved studying American history. I particularly enjoyed research projects involving original source materials. Most of those materials with which I worked were located at the Ohio Historical Society, which had original papers from all sorts of historical figures. I would use those materials as a basis to write research reports and papers. I found that an overwhelming sense of responsibility accompanies the project when writing a historical paper. It dawned on me that *I am writing a history paper about this, and somebody is going to read it.* The author has a responsibility to get it right. It is tough because how do you figure out what really happened? Many events took place a long time ago, so conjecture was tempting. I learned to drill down through the source materials and focus on presenting ideas in a factual way with minimal conscious bias.

One lengthy paper concerned the 1944 presidential campaign of Ohio Governor John W. Bricker, a legendary figure in American and Ohio political history. (Bricker did not ultimately win the presidential nomination but became the vice-presidential nominee on the 1944 Republican ticket led by New York Governor Thomas E. Dewey, who lost to President Franklin D. Roosevelt in his bid for a fourth term.) I interviewed Governor (later Senator) Bricker several times and supplemented the information from those interviews with plentiful original materials from the archives of the Ohio Historical Society, including internal campaign correspondence and a large collection of news reports. We spoke at length about his experiences during the campaign as well as the two wings of the Republican Party that were dominant at the time of his candidacy (East Coast/Wall Street versus Midwest/Main Street). The need for accuracy weighed heavily on me, especially because many of the people involved were still alive. I omitted no material information and had to make sure what I wrote was correct.

I felt the same sense of responsibility when researching and writing my senior dissertation on John F. Kennedy and the McCarthy controversy, under the inspired guidance of Professor Reichard, whose insightful scholarship and positive attitude had a major influence on my appreciation of history and higher education. In the 1950s, Senator Joseph R. McCarthy (R-Wis.) stirred public tension with accusations of widespread communist infiltration of the United States government. He developed a devoted following in many places, including the Commonwealth of Massachusetts, which a young John F. Kennedy was then representing in the United States Senate. McCarthy's popularity in Massachusetts and close personal ties to the Kennedy family put Kennedy in a bind when the Senate took up a resolution to censure McCarthy after the Army–McCarthy hearings of 1954. To the disappointment of many liberals and others, Senator Kennedy abstained during recuperation from back surgery.

My research for the senior dissertation involved the use of voluminous original materials from the Kennedy Library's archives and interviews with many people who had worked with then-Senator Kennedy (including Theodore C. Sorensen, Ambassador Henry Cabot Lodge, Senator Leverett A. Saltonstall, and Roy M. Cohn, among others). As with the Bricker paper, what guided me was the need to get it right so history would treat the individuals involved fairly. Mr. Sorensen asked me to send him a copy of my completed dissertation, which I did, and this made me even more scrupulous in substantiating what I wrote. It was a special privilege to talk with him, in view of the many years he had spent as one of JFK's closest confidants during the Senate and White House years. The opportunity for a personal interview with Roy Cohn was also especially valuable, given the integral and controversial role he had played as chief counsel to Senator McCarthy and the vivid memories he retained.

The senior dissertation was ideal training for the study and practice of law as a litigator. Most lawsuits involve a reconstruction of events. The parties normally have different recollections of what happened or different positions as to what rule of law applies. When analyzing a case in the classroom to understand its legal principles, it is essential to grasp the key facts and procedural posture of the matter at hand. The same is true in guiding an active lawsuit to an appropriate conclusion. In a trial court, it is the job of the trier of fact (a judge or jury) to determine the truth, either beyond a reasonable doubt (in criminal cases) or by the preponderance of the evidence or clear and convincing evidence (the most common standards in civil cases). In an appellate court, the judges focus on the governing legal standard and look to the trial court proceedings to determine whether there is a suitable record to apply it. Resourcefulness and painstaking attention to factual details and the relevant case law allow an attorney to be more persuasive in either context. Undergraduate research papers require the same skills for successful preparation.

Life on Campus

Thanks to the Joyce Scholarship, I lived on campus all four years. For the first two years, there were four of us in one room. In addition to adjusting to the close quarters of the crowded dormitories (made easier by having decent roommates and neighbors), there was also the need to adapt to a wide variety of lifestyles. Even though Ohio State is situated in the same city in which I grew up and is a land-grant university in the Midwest, it felt different to live there and was like being far away from home. The student body came mostly from Ohio. There were several students from the East Coast and a few from overseas.

My academic inclinations carried over from high school, and I ended up studying a lot. The occasional late-nighters of high school evolved into more frequent all-nighters in college as I prepared for tests or wrote research papers. I knew I wanted to go to law school. Admission to law school was extremely limited, so the circumstances required it. On more than one occasion I would finish a paper at dawn, slide it under the professor's door, then have doughnuts for breakfast on the Oval (the center of the campus) and carry on with the day. In addition to the academic work, I gravitated naturally to the OSU Pre-Law Club and ultimately served as its president.

The college years were also a time of great social growth. Many of my friends were other young men who were interested in going to law school or into government or business after graduation, so we were all in the same boat. In an era when full-fledged participation by women in the economy was not nearly as widespread as it is today, it was a new experience to get to know extraordinary women who were also pursuing careers in not only law but also health sciences and hospital records management, architecture, landscaping, women's studies, and other occupations.

Over summer vacations I had to work, and I wanted to use the time as constructively as possible. One summer, I was able to get a job at the Supreme Court of Ohio Law Library, working with Dr. Paul S. Fu and a crew of other college students in moving the law library and Supreme Court justices' chambers from the Statehouse Annex to a new office tower across the street. The job provided daily exposure to the highly specialized sorts of books and journals a law library contains and gave me a foretaste of subjects I hoped to study one day in law school. Dr. Fu, whose family was said to have been aboard the last train out of China before the communist takeover in the late 1940s, was dedicated as director to efficient management of the library and insisted on punctuality. He often would stand by the door at 1:00 p.m. to make sure we understood a one-hour lunch break meant one hour. He also was ahead of his time as a manager. Underscoring the emergence of women in the traditionally male-dominated workplace, it was the first time (in several of our projects) I worked under the supervision of a woman who was about the same age as me.

The next two summers, I worked at the Public Utilities Commission of Ohio with (once again) Dr. Sweet, whom Governor Gilligan had named to the commission. Much of my work involved research on how public utility regulation could accommodate new technology, energy demands, and repercussions of the OPEC oil embargo.

During my academic years, for other ways to earn spending money, I also worked as a tutor in history and political science for the OSU football team, a front desk clerk at a campus area hotel, an assistant at the OSU Archives, and a field interviewer for the Academy for Contemporary Problems. The work as a football team tutor was as interesting as the opportunity to get to know the athletes in that context. My job was to meet with the team members who had upcoming tests in history or political science. I was impressed with how disciplined they were about their studies, prompted in part by the frequent presence of Coach Woody Hayes, who would walk up and down the aisles of the study hall. A historian and World War II veteran, Coach Hayes would occasionally stop by the table and offer his own insight into the matters at hand.

My interest in student politics continued at college. I became involved in the undergraduate student government during my senior year, winning election to the student assembly and becoming president pro tempore. In that capacity, a year or so after President Nixon's near-impeachment and resignation, I presided over the impeachment trial of the president of our student government over expenditure issues. The experience showed me the importance of fairness, impartiality, and integrity in handling such a responsibility—and the extraordinary pressure such a situation puts on all involved.

Studying at Oxford University in England

In my freshman year at Ohio State, I saw a flyer announcing a new program that would enable students to study at Oxford University in England for the summer. It immediately struck me as a distinctive opportunity because of the preeminence of Oxford University and the chance to spend a useful summer overseas. I applied to participate. However, there was a cost attached, and even though I was on a scholarship at college, I had little spare cash. The only way I could afford to go would be to sell my car—a yellow Pontiac Firebird. I managed to get $900 for it and, with that and a small loan, had enough to go. Our group of several dozen undergraduates left the United States in early July 1973 and stayed in Oxford until the end of August.

The program was called English History, Literature, and Art from 1760 to 1840 and was housed at one of the Oxford colleges. I was initially disappointed when I learned we were going to be based at New College because I wanted to see and experience the Oxford traditions in a historic environment, and I assumed from the name that New College was a more contemporary addition. I was wrong. New College, as it turned out, was actually founded in 1379.

Upon our arrival, when I saw where we were and what we would be doing, I knew right away it would have been a huge mistake not to have come. I was so glad I had taken the risk of enrolling. Oxford University is steeped in history and dedicated to excellence. It draws students from around the world. The many centuries of its existence vastly expanded my concept of time, having grown up in Columbus, where most of our oldest buildings and institutions date back only to the 1850s and 1860s. I had vacillated about going—the decision to sell my car at that age and go abroad for a first-time program was not easy—but the minute I got there, it was clear the choice was right.

We lived within the walled grounds of New College, walked through the cloister adjoining the chapel, and ate in the medieval dining hall every day. It was completely absorbing, a whole new world for me. The coursework focused on the period that corresponded with the American Revolution and its aftermath. We looked at those events through a British lens. Learning the history from a British perspective gave me a better understanding of the independence movement in the American colonies. The art was a big revelation. I had never really been exposed to art, so I was unaccustomed to it. The literature was also new to me. William Wordsworth was one of the poets we studied, and on the weekends, we visited some of the places about which he wrote, such as Tintern Abbey.

The classes were taught differently—most of them by tutorials. We were given materials to read and assignments to complete; then, we met in small groups or individually with the instructor and presented our work. That was new to me, as I was more acquainted with the larger-scale classes (with exams) that are customary in the United States. Even without grades (because it was a summer program), the tutorial system was demanding. We had to be able to talk about what we had done—what we had studied—and defend our conclusions and opinions. The available resources were enormous, from vast libraries to talented faculty members. The other people in the program also enriched the experience. Most of us were undergraduates at Ohio State. There were also students from other colleges and universities. They brought a wide range of perspectives and experiences.

Introduction to the English Channel

Outside the walls of New College was one additional learning experience that would inspire me decades afterward. Several fellow students and I traveled around Britain on the weekends. The excursion that had the most enduring impact on me was the night we camped on the cliffs at Dover that overlook the English Channel. From the top of Shakespeare Cliff during daylight, I wrote at the time, "I beheld the most beautiful sight I've ever seen in my life. I could see for miles and miles out into the Channel and along the coast; the weather, warm and sunny and windy, was perfect." The view that night "was simply spectacular. A nearly full white moon reflected on the water, and the clear sky was full of stars. The air was somewhat chilly but very fresh. Many ships at sea sailed through the English Channel below us all night." The next morning, I "walked for hours atop the cliffs" and "came across some bunkers used in the Second World War by the English and crawled into one." My mind raced as I imagined what it would have been like for the defenders, especially during the most desperate days of the war.

I also wondered what it would be like to swim the English Channel. The distance across to France is twenty-one miles. Some days the French coast is visible from the English shore; other days it is not. The water is cold, generally ranging from fifty-seven to sixty-three degrees Fahrenheit (thirteen to seventeen degrees Celsius). Sometimes, the water is calm; other times, it is rough, depending on the wind. A strong tide flows through the Channel twice daily.

Four decades later, still inspired by that curiosity, I returned as captain of three separate relay teams that swam the English Channel, starting from Dover near Shakespeare Cliff and crossing to the French shore. Each team had six swimmers, including me. The first team commemorated the seventieth anniversary of D-Day in 2014. We called that team Overlord 70, based on the name of the D-Day operation. The second team marked the one hundredth anniversary in 2017 of the arrival of the American troops in France for World War I and was called Over There!, reminiscent of the popular song of that time. The third team, also in 2017, was named Overcome in honor of the anthem of the American civil rights movement. All three teams successfully crossed the chilly waters of the channel without wetsuits (in two of the crossings, we swam through the night) in rotating one-hour increments. For me, each swim was as awesome as I had imagined while camping overnight on Shakespeare Cliff in the summer of 1973.

I was sad to leave Oxford at the end of such a life-changing experience that summer. My camping classmates from Shakespeare Cliff and I went over to the Continent for two weeks afterward, to France, Belgium, the Netherlands, and Switzerland. I set off one day before the others, taking a ferry from Dover to Calais and then riding the train to Paris. It was the first time I had ever been to a place where English was not the predominant language. I could not speak French, so communication with people I met was limited. I remember sitting instead in the Place de la Concorde—the large public square in the heart of Paris—after buying a bottle of wine and a ham sandwich and having an impromptu dinner there on my own. It felt like being in the center of the world.

The Oxford summer experience profoundly shaped my future. The trip was my first time outside the United States, at about the same age as my father when his service in the military likewise changed his life. Oxford is such a legendary university. What I saw there—the emphasis placed on knowledge—made me even more serious about education. I saw that education did not make someone better than anyone else, but it did provide skills and perspectives that could be useful for solving problems. The caliber of education at Oxford was beyond anything I had previously imagined and set a new standard for me when I got back to Ohio State that fall, which would lead me to aim even higher when I applied to law school.

Graduation

In my remaining three years at Ohio State, I focused with greater intensity on going to law school. I graduated in June 1976. My experience as a Buckeye dispelled for me one myth about enrolling in such a large public institution—that it supposedly relegates the student to becoming lost in the crowd. On the contrary, I saw that the university had enormous resources at its disposal, especially in terms of talented faculty members who were eager to help students who sought them out, and a wide array of courses. It required more initiative on the part of the students than may have been involved elsewhere, but it proved to me the proposition that where there's a will, there's a way in the context of the public university system.

After graduation, two friends and I took a road trip to California. I returned to Columbus to work again that summer for Dr. Sweet on research projects at the Public Utilities Commission of Ohio and prepare for the next step ahead—law school.

Chapter 4:
Yale Law School

I do not remember a time after my early grade school years when I did not want to become a lawyer. Most of the figures in American history I admired had been lawyers, and it struck me as the kind of occupation I was cut out for because I liked learning and advocacy and responsibility for protecting others. However, I did not know any lawyers; nobody in my family had been in the legal profession.

Applying for Law School

Most of what I knew about the process of becoming a lawyer consisted of stories about how difficult it was to get into law school. It was essential to get high grades and take a standardized admission test. That gave me a strong motivation. I knew I would have to do well in grade school, high school, and then college. A popular movie that came out in 1973, *The Paper Chase*, which portrayed the challenges faced by a first-year student at Harvard Law School, ironically made law school seem even more appealing to me.

At the beginning of my senior year, I did not limit my future to law school. Because graduation would be such a crossroads moment, I also considered becoming a historian and took the Graduate Record Exam, contemplated going into the diplomatic corps and took the US Foreign Service exam, and applied for a Rhodes Scholarship. But none of those alternatives evolved beyond those preliminary stages.

I talked about law school with as many people as I could find who were familiar with the admissions process, and I looked into courses various law schools offered and how to afford the tuition and room and board.

When I chose my undergraduate college, I had the benefit of having lived on the Ohio State campus during the Ohio Governor's School program and was lucky to have received a full scholarship, which made college affordable for me. When it came to applying for law school, I also had had the experience of studying, if only briefly, at Oxford. I saw things from a different perspective and wanted to look more broadly.

Law school applications were similar to their college counterparts, with essays and questions. Yale was one of the last schools to which I applied because its deadline was later. Instead of writing an essay for the Yale application, as I had done for every other law school, I wrote a lengthy autobiographical poem. The verses almost wrote themselves as I sat at the typewriter. I remember only the first two lines: "Comes now before you John, a male / Who hopes to study law at Yale." Taking the risk of being unconventional, I included the poem with the application and sent the package off to Yale.

I applied for admission to Yale and other law schools in the fall of 1975. During Thanksgiving vacation that year, I spent time traveling and visiting schools to which I had applied, including Yale in New Haven, Connecticut. A classmate from the Oxford program who went to Yale Law School after college invited me to stay with him and his wife when I was in New Haven, and they showed me around and introduced me to people in their class. Upon meeting their classmates, I knew that if I were fortunate enough to be admitted, Yale was where I wanted to study law. There were a lot of kindred spirits there, and I thought I could maximize my growth in such an environment. The students came from many walks of life and all around the nation and struck me as unpretentious and interested in learning, virtues not exclusive to Yale Law School but which I found there in abundance.

Since then, I have advised people applying for college or law school to schedule their visits for days when students will be on campus because the class they would be in is likely to be similar to the one they find during their visit. Classes tend to replicate themselves, so if you can see yourself in such a setting, you probably *will* feel it appropriate for you to be there when it is your turn.

Early in April 1976, after spring break, I was back on campus at Ohio State. At the time I was living in Baker Hall. There was a message at the front desk one night when I got back from studying. "Call home," it said. I rang, and my mother answered. She was excited. "Johnny," she said, "there's an envelope for you here. It's a big envelope from Yale." It was always a positive sign if it was a big envelope rather than a small envelope, back in the days when schools notified applicants by mail, so I asked if she would open it. As my mother put down the phone and opened the envelope, I could hear her cheer in the background, so I knew it was good news. "It is my pleasure to inform you that you have been approved for admission to the Yale Law School class of 1979" the letter said in its opening sentence. My mother was beyond thrilled for me, and I was delighted too. I sent in the deposit right away.

Arriving at Yale Law School

The law school dean, Harry H. Wellington, set the tone for the three years ahead in a letter he sent to the class before the school year got underway. He wrote in the aftermath of the Watergate scandal, in which the Nixon administration's attempt to conceal its involvement in a burglary of the Democratic National Committee headquarters led to the downfall of the president and incarceration of several officials who were lawyers. As Dean Wellington noted, "The past few years have made us witness to the worst, and the best, of law in action. We have seen lawyers drawn into excess in pursuit of public and private causes; and other lawyers sounding the grandest themes known to our republic as they play out their roles in Congress, the courts, and counsel for state and accused." He reminded us that "no other profession is tested so insistently, and so visibly, by the temptations of power and none owes as great a moral obligation to use that power creatively and wisely. We confront a future in which the potential abuse of power will continue to be very much on people's minds."

The night I arrived at Yale in September 1976, after taking the train from Columbus, I took my belongings to my room. My new roommate—Charles W. "Chip" Fournier—had already arrived from Texas, and his luggage was in the room. He was not there, but I saw he had a cap from the San Antonio Polo Club, which was quite different from my own circumstances. A few minutes later, the first classmate whom I actually met had just returned from a position on the faculty at Cambridge University in England. I started to feel in way over my head. The law school was full of people like them—I met one after another—but, as it turned out, was an egalitarian place. People tended to respect and accept each other, whatever their background may be.

I received a partial scholarship that, with loans and earnings from summer jobs, helped me pay for tuition and room and board. One feature of the class I had not fully anticipated was the breadth of circumstances from which we came. Two examples, just from New York: One of my classmates grew up on Park Avenue and was extraordinarily wealthy; meanwhile, another grew up in the projects in the Bronx (she is now Justice Sonia Sotomayor). Beyond the socioeconomic spread, there were people from around the world. One such student was Mpazi Sinjela, from Zambia, who lived in my dorm corridor one year and opened my eyes to a part of the world I would come to love after law school.

Some of my fellow students had taken time off from their studies or pursued other careers before starting law school, whereas I came straight from college. I never felt that was a disadvantage. One-third of the class members were women, which was significant for that day and age. It was an example of Yale Law School blending long-accepted tradition with fresh creative thinking. I quickly learned to think for myself in that context and not simply accept conventional wisdom. Our objective was to get to the bottom of things. We had no need to accept the status quo.

The day before classes started, as I sat in the courtyard, it occurred to me: *This is for . . . forever.* I had hoped for a long time to have a future as a lawyer. Up to then, the academic years had progressed on a quarter-by-quarter basis; when one quarter was over, its classes would be behind me, and then would come the next quarter and different subjects. The rhythm and pace of the continuous change were comfortable. But when I started law school, it was exceedingly clear it was a long-term proposition and a turning point that would set the course for the rest of my life. I took in my surroundings, watching the other students mill around this venerated seat of learning—literally on the eve of law school—knowing this was it. This would be forever, and the realization was almost overwhelming. I felt prepared but surprised at how permanent my entry into the legal profession suddenly seemed to be.

Professors and Peers

I was at Yale Law School from September 1976 through June 1979. There was a major emphasis on social justice in our curriculum because of the history unfolding around us. Several faculty members had served in leading roles in the civil rights movement and other historic events. All the faculty members had considerable academic pedigrees and distinctive ways of teaching. In many ways, however, the Watergate Affair had set the stage for the study of law in the late 1970s. Lawyers who had been derelict of their duty bore much responsibility for the unlawful events that had transpired. It was a time of reckoning for the legal profession itself.

Arthur Leff, my contracts professor, was a brilliant man. Listening to him was always a captivating experience. Professor Leff was the sort of person who made us want to absorb every word of what he was saying. Contracts became unusually interesting under his guidance. Even more fortunately, his contracts class was the one I had for "small group." Although the dozen or so of us in the class took all our other first-semester courses together with several other similar groups, we had the contracts class with Professor Leff all to ourselves.

Among my other teachers and classes were Professors Joe Bishop (torts and business units), Ralph Brown (environmental law), Guido Calabresi (tort issues), Marvin Chirelstein (federal income tax), Elias Clark (estates and property), Robert Clark (financial institutions), Robert Cover (civil procedure), Steven Duke (criminal procedure), Owen Fiss (injunctions), Paul Gewirtz (legislation), Quinton Johnstone (property), Eugene Rostow (international law), Barbara Underwood (criminal law), and Ralph Winter (constitutional law).

One professor who made an especially lasting impression was Bruce Ackerman. He taught several courses on constitutional theory and social justice. On our final day in his social justice class, his closing point was that, as lawyers, our job would be to "domesticate the intractable reality." That remark immediately embedded itself in my mind and has guided me in the practice of law ever since. When arguing or settling a case, it is imperative to figure out not only my side but also the other side. What is the irreducible essence? What is the rock bottom? What are the immutable facts of life we all must deal with? After that, everything else tends to fall into place.

I learned an enormous amount from everybody at the law school with me. As is common in law school, students can absorb at least as much from their classmates as from the faculty. Yale Law School made a deliberate effort to draw students from a wide range of backgrounds and locations. Just by associating with our peers, we were bound to learn a lot. It was eye-opening to encounter situations and groups to which I had never before been exposed. There were people from all different backgrounds—students from all around the nation and many different schools, including military academies, and a breadth of circumstances. It showed me how much there was to learn . . . and to avoid being presumptuous. There is much to be said for intuition, but carefully listening to *others'* thoughts and experiences is how to truly grow.

Our class itself was relatively small, with only about 160 students, so we all were acquainted with each other to some degree. Whenever we pick back up, the time and distance fade away. One site of many late-night conversations at the time was the Law Library. It was open around the clock and frequented at all hours of the day. Two fellow students and I were often there into the early morning hours and struck up what became lifelong friendships in the course of many nocturnal conversations. They were Gary and Robert Katzmann, twin brothers from Queens, New York, who were separated by one year at law school.

The warm spring evenings were the source of my most lasting acoustic memory of Yale Law School. I lived in the dormitory part of the law school quadrangle all three years. For two of those years, the windows of my rooms faced out onto the quad. When the weather was nice, many of us would open our windows to catch the fresh air. Late at night, I could hear fellow students who, like me, were typing away diligently, in an era when we all had manual typewriters. Typing required great patience because if there were an error that could not be "whited out," the whole page had to be torn out and restarted. But the staccato clacking of countless keystrokes, the dinging of carriage returns, and the pulling of completed pages were sounds of progress that have remained a pleasant memory.

The Yale Law Journal

The law journal was a big part of my life. I learned much from serving as an editor; it was one of the parts of law school I enjoyed the most. I assumed when I applied for the law journal that it was going to be an intense and focused writing experience, which proved to be the case. The responsibilities of an editor were to help review proposed publications, carefully vet them, and assist in editing the ones the law journal accepted for publication. Alongside those tasks, we were each writing something ourselves.

The way to become a member of *The Yale Law Journal* at the time was to have a "note" (an extended analytic essay about a specific case or issue) accepted for publication. Students applied by presenting their proposed note at the end of the first year; then, they worked through an editing process with the incumbent editors. If the note was accepted (ordinarily at the beginning of the second year), the author would become a member of the law journal. My note was accepted, so the law journal became my major extracurricular activity in my second and third years.

The title was "Equal Representation of Party Members on Political Party Central Committees." The Supreme Court of the United States had issued a series of rulings in the mid-1960s that required apportionment of legislative bodies on the basis of what was then called "one man, one vote." Every district had to have a substantially equal number of people so the people of every district would have the same degree of representation. One sort of governing body to which courts had not widely applied the concept by the late 1970s was the political party central committee.

In most states, central committees govern political parties and perform important functions, including the selection of public officials in some instances. The laws of many states specified that the central committees must consist of an equal number of committee persons from each district. When party affiliation varies among districts that have an equal number of central committee members, an imbalance results. Some districts with few Democrats, for example, would have the same representation as districts with heavy Democratic majorities. As a result, party members might be either overrepresented or underrepresented on the central committee. My note examined ways in which courts should apply the "one person, one vote" principle to political party central committees.

Reapportionment was a major issue in American law at the time because the nation was still in the first generation of "one person, one vote" representation. So, when I submitted my draft note, it filtered its way through the law journal process. The editor assigned to me was Matthew T. Heartney, who was in the class ahead of me. He was thorough and probing. He asked insightful questions—ones that never would have occurred to me—and raised points about the reapportionment decisions and the operation of political party central committees I was taking for granted. His editorial oversight proved to be highly productive. *The Yale Law Journal* published my note in volume 88 in 1978.

There was one unexpected postscript. A year after we graduated, my friend and law journal colleague Peter Canfield called and said, "Guess what? The Supreme Court just cited your note in one of its opinions!" I was pleasantly surprised; Justice John P. Stevens had actually cited my note in his opinion for the Supreme Court in the case called *Marchioro v. Chaney*. Many years later, when I met Justice Stevens, I thanked him for doing that. He remembered the case but, unsurprisingly, not my note.

The law journal gave me a lot of experience in editing draft materials, polishing manuscripts, and analyzing court opinions. The first time I wrote a lengthy piece for publication, in college several years before, the process had been excruciating. It seemed to take forever. I would start out thinking, *This ought to be easy; I am just writing down what I know.* But it was difficult, and I had to acknowledge I might not know as much as I thought I did or how to express it clearly. But with the law journal experience, I became accustomed to that sort of challenge and got comfortable with the demands and frustrations it involves. Over the years, my cases have involved a lot of research and writing. My career would have been different if I had not developed that skill.

The editing work on the law journal also involved checking the citations to manuscripts. This was before electronic citation checking, so when an author had cited cases or other sources in a draft article, we had to actually pull each of the books off the law library shelves and put them all on a long table in a back room. Then, we would go through them one by one, opening the books, finding the references, and double-checking the quotations and citations. Thankfully, the process has become immensely more efficient over time.

The quarters in which the law journal was situated had their own charm—tucked away in a tiny, cramped space amid the library stacks. There were low ceilings and towers of books and loose papers everywhere, with heating pipes clanking around us. A thin haze of cigarette smoke permeated the offices. I loved the no-frills atmosphere. The law journal now has orderly offices with windows and sunshine, no smoking, fresh paint, polished floors, bright lights, and a chronological array of the group photographs of the editors of each volume in the hallway.

Life Outside the Classroom

Law school was not all work. We were all busy with coursework but still made time to get together, at lunch or dinner or on trips down to New York from time to time. My dormitory friends and neighbors Fred Biesecker, Peter Canfield, Chip Fournier, Peter Kougasian, Peter Lancaster, George "Nibs" Nelson, and Dick Tyner, among others, were among my most frequent mealtime and weekend companions.

There was also a popular film society. On Fridays and Saturdays, the society would show previously released movies in the law school auditorium.

We now take for granted that we can sit down with our laptop computers and, in just a few minutes, find almost any movie we want to see, but it was not like that back then. The film societies were great resources for watching movies we had not seen before and spending time with each other. I do not recall if *The Paper Chase*, which had inspired me in college, was one of the movies the society showed. By coincidence, though, I became acquainted at Yale with John Jay Osborne Jr., the author of the book on which the movie was based, who was a graduate law student and occupant of one of the dorm rooms in which I subsequently lived.

For exercise, the Grove Street Cemetery, across the street behind the law school, provided ideal gravel running paths, past the shaded graves of illustrious Americans such as Eli Whitney (inventor of the cotton gin), Noah Webster (of dictionary fame), Roger Sherman (Revolution-era statesman), and others. The nearby Payne Whitney Gym had two pools, including the first fifty-meter pool in which I ever swam.

Grades and Graduation

One unusual thing about Yale Law School was that we did not have standard grades. Our performance in every course was evaluated on a pass-fail basis, with the possibility of getting an honors mark. That system gave us the opportunity to focus on areas of special interest while learning the fundamentals, putting a premium on the intrinsic incentive to do well and making everything more self-motivated. There were four or five students who were so exceptionally smart that they were incomparable, literally. The rest of us were capable, but I did not sense a lot of competition. For me, it was three good years in an inspiring atmosphere with a focus on working, engaging in public service, getting jobs, and figuring out what my career would be. I was overwhelmingly fortunate to go there and loved virtually every minute of it.

I graduated from Yale Law School in June 1979, at a ceremony distinguished by the commencement address of Professor Leon Lipson. His address was composed exclusively of one-syllable words. The Ohio bar exam awaited me. One other big difference about going to a law school like Yale was that the curriculum did not prepare us to take any particular state's bar exam. As a result, we enjoyed the freedom and benefit of broader thinking during our law school years. But we paid a price when the time came to take our bar exams, which involved a lot of intense catch-up studying to learn about state law on subjects we had not covered in law school. A crash course in secured transactions just weeks before the bar exam was typical of that nerve-racking process for me, especially because I was studying on my own in Nashville, during a judicial clerkship, without access to the in-person group study bar exam courses being offered in Ohio. The risk was not lost upon me in the process.

My graduation from Yale Law School, June 1979.

Chapter 5:
On the Ground in Africa

A law school friendship led me to Africa a year after graduation. Mpazi Sinjela was a graduate law student from Zambia. He lived down the hall in the law school dorm. Mpazi mentioned one day that his aunt was secretary-general of the trade unions in Zambia. The more I thought about that, the more it amazed me. I knew so little about Africa. It dawned upon me that if there were trade unions, then there were industries, and if there were industries, there must be banks and infrastructure and highways and schools and all sorts of institutions. Of course, all that should have been obvious to me. I became intrigued enough to want to go to Africa and learn firsthand about its legal and political systems.

After graduation I worked for the summer at Jones, Day, Reavis & Pogue, a large law firm based in Cleveland, Ohio. Then, from August 1979 to August 1980, I served as a law clerk for Judge Gilbert S. Merritt Jr. of the United States Court of Appeals for the Sixth Circuit. With those two jobs under my belt, I had saved enough money to travel on a shoestring budget. The law firm at which I was planning to work in Columbus said I could delay my start until January 1981. So I set off for Cairo in August 1980 with just a backpack, $2,000 worth of traveler's checks plus some cash in my pocket, a passport full of visas, and a return plane ticket from Cape Town at the end of December. It was a huge risk, especially on a low budget, but the challenge of discovery and doing something difficult attracted me.

Cairo to Kilimanjaro

The adventure got off to an unusual start aboard the transatlantic flight from New York to London in late August 1980. My seatmate and I had a long conversation during the early part of the flight. He was a rugged but well-to-do middle-aged industrial developer on his way to Nigeria, where he was going to supervise the construction of a sugar plantation. He had been to Africa many times and had several tales to tell. Unfortunately, for a new traveler like me, most of his stories were worrisome. He emphasized only the dangers of African travel and gave me several stern warnings. Especially unsettling was his advice about the first two countries on my itinerary. "Don't sail on the dhows up the Nile in Egypt," he said, referring to the traditional sailboats. "The pilots are known to rob their passengers and then throw them off into the river to drown." Pointing to my new hiking boots, he said, "There are Sudanese who would kill for shoes like those." He then went soundly to sleep.

Unable to do the same after what he had just told me, and since I was such a novice passenger, I asked a flight attendant if it might be possible to go up to the cockpit for a while. That did not seem like such an audacious request at the time, but it is a true sign we live now in a completely different era, when such a question would be unthinkable. The pilot said yes, and he and the crew let me stay with them for a long time. All seemed quiet outside. Except for the motion of our airliner relative to the few ships illuminated below, it was nearly impossible from that vantage point to sense that we were moving. We seemed suspended in the night sky. The pilot and navigator pointed out the stars and planets that surrounded us. They also explained the effect of the winds on our travel time and many other aspects of jet transportation and were interested in what I was setting out to do in Africa. After that, I returned to my seat and was able to sleep the rest of the way to London.

Following a day in London, I flew to Cairo in the evening. A blast of heat filled the plane when the door opened. As I stepped off the aircraft and looked down the stairway to the tarmac, I saw a gauntlet of soldiers that led from the foot of the stairs to the door of the airport, with fixed bayonets thrust upward. The stern glares of the white-garbed troops kept the other arriving passengers and me under close observation as we walked through the cordon in the scorching desert air.

The harsh welcome proved to be a sharp contrast to the four months of colorful adventure ahead of me in Africa. Cairo is in the north of

Africa, in Egypt, and Cape Town is at the far southern tip of the continent, in South Africa. I had to get visas ahead of time, which was complicated because it involved paperwork for Egypt, Sudan, Kenya, Uganda, Tanzania, Zambia, Zimbabwe, and South Africa. A lot of vaccinations also were required, as was a regimen of malaria-prevention pills. There were only two deadlines to meet. First, I wanted to climb Mount Kilimanjaro, which is best done before the rainy season begins in Tanzania. That was coming in the middle of November 1980, so I had to be there by the beginning of November. The other deadline was the plane home from Cape Town at the end of December to be back for Christmas 1980 and the start of my new job in January. But that was it; everything else developed on a day-to-day basis. It became a challenge to move on from any given spot because nearly everywhere I went was intensely interesting, and I would happily have stayed much longer.

Although I flew to Cairo by myself, I started meeting other travelers right away and was almost always with somebody. A lot of young Israelis were traveling at the time. If I had an opportunity to travel with them, I would, because they almost all had served in the military in Israel and were accustomed to the rigors and risks of travel. Most of them were avid adventurers who shared the philosophy of "learning the world through your feet." It was fun to travel with such intrepid and motivated people.

Walks through Cairo became an immersion in the ancient (the pyramids and the Sphinx) and the medieval. Back streets were filled with people dressed as they would have been in biblical times, with countless donkeys and goats but hardly any cars on the narrow roads. Instead, children rode by at the reins of donkey carts. Small manufacturing enterprises were strung along the alleys. In one house, for example, people would heat iron, which their neighbors in the next house would cool and the residents of the next dwelling would store. The same process appeared to be used for the manufacture and assembly of furniture.

Cairo was my introduction to the Islamic faith and culture. I arrived during Ramadan, the lunar month during which Muslims fast during the day and devote extra time to prayer and family. That observance required quick adaptation on my part, as most restaurants and food vendors were closed during daylight hours. It was the first time I had ever heard the prayer calls, known as the adhan and chanted in Arabic, broadcast from minarets at five specified times of the day, starting with first light and ending in late evening. I visited mosques large and small. I learned to remove my shoes upon entering, then wash my hands and feet at the entryway fountain and respect the faithful as they worshipped, separated by gender, in a ritual sequence of motions and silently repeated prayers. Inside, the quiet and carpet-laden mosques were a peaceful refuge from the constant noise, blazing heat, and glaring sun outside.

After taking a train to Luxor and a boat from Aswan, I crossed into Sudan at Wadi Halfa. The crowded passenger boat moved steadily for two days up Lake Nasser, created by the Aswan Dam, drifting past the sprawling sand embankments. Onboard, several English-speaking travelers and I spent the days on the open-air top deck talking and listening to the BBC World News. I remember particularly reports about the change of government in Poland. The new leader was the Soviet-backed communist Stanislaw Kania. I recall the broadcasts and the mention of his name because of the urgency with which the BBC announcer articulated the situation. Our Sudan-bound packet seemed like a world away from Central Europe, but the radio connected us directly with the drama unfolding there. When darkness fell, we spent the nights on the top deck stargazing into the clear sky above us. I had never seen the sky as clear or star studded as then.

Upon landing at Wadi Halfa, the sun was searing, broiling the brown Sudanese sand, as I got onboard an old train that traveled slowly across the vast desert from there to Khartoum. A sandstorm at night made it hard to breathe, except through a scarf, and difficult to see down the corridor of the train car. Eventually, the storm let up, and we encountered tea vendors under the stars at the desolate train stops. Faithful Muslims took the opportunity to engage in the prayer ritual along the way during the daytime, unrolling prayer rugs onto the desert sand and hastening the prayer when the train whistle signaled our imminent departure.

When I arrived in Khartoum, the capital, I went to the Supreme Court building and asked about the justices, looking in particular for any judge with a connection to Yale Law School. That approach was productive. I met the deputy chief justice of the Supreme Court of Sudan and Justice Hassan Ali Hamad, who spoke with me about the Koran, the definitive text of the Islamic faith and one of the bases of Sharia law, the Islamic legal system. In Juba I met Justice Wilson Aryamba, who also was serving on the Supreme Court of Sudan. He invited me to lunch, and we had a deeply interesting conversation. The main point was his emphasis on the writ of habeas corpus as the most important power of any court, as it gives the court the ability to bring forth somebody who has been imprisoned and make the government justify why it is holding them. At the time there was a dictatorship in Sudan, with few other controls on who was locked up, so he taught me in an eminently practical way about the importance of the writ.

After several days in Khartoum and a visit to the large and heartrending Ethiopian refugee camp at Um Gulga, I made my way to the south of Sudan in a series of trains and truck beds. I would often sit on top of the train. It was hot inside, and the train had to go slowly because of the aged state of the tracks. Many passengers climbed up and sat on top of the cars. People seemed more at ease and willing to talk with me up there than they would have been inside the carriage—presumably because no one was likely to overhear them.

I was on a train to Wau when we crossed the invisible line that separates North Africa, where the population is largely Arab and Islamic, from the rest of Africa, which is populated mostly by Black people who practice Christianity or other forms of spirituality. There is a marked cultural difference. A couple of miles out from Malual, one of the first villages on the Black African side, we could hear people waiting to welcome the train. I wrote at the time that I "awoke to singing dancers with spears and yellow and red clothing as the train passed" and saw "dignified young warriors in loincloths along the tracks." People started beating drums amid a joyful commotion; they lined the tracks and offered sugar cane and other such commodities as the train slowly made its way to the station, bringing their families and friends back from the north. It was an emotional and sentimental homecoming for many passengers.

The truck ride that followed between Wau and Juba was a further immersion into the hospitality of the Sudanese people. At a fare of around five dollars for a six-day trip, I rode in the back of a large truck, nestled among soldiers, nursing women, children, fellow wayfarers, and a host of small animals. The going was slow, the roads often just dirt paths through the savanna. At one point, when we reached a bridge that had been washed out, everyone got off and crossed the stream by foot, with women carrying babies over their heads before the unloaded truck crossed the streambed safely. Meanwhile, that day, while waiting with empty stomachs for the driver to assess the situation, several of us found the nearby village of a chief and were given roasted peanuts and a pumpkin-like mash to eat. We also improvised on at least one evening, when we simply stopped where the truck ended up at nightfall and slept in the straw field.

Being outdoors for such long stretches of time was refreshing, especially after I had been leading a studious indoor lifestyle for years. To be in the open air continuously for several days affected me in ways I had not expected. I began to blend in with things—almost literally. After riding in the back of the truck for nearly a week, when we finally reached a village where there was a shower, I stood under the flowing water, watching myself shed dirt that turned into a thin layer of mud around the drain. It felt great.

I was able to get exposure to the practice of Catholicism in Africa, starting in Sudan. I met several of the missionaries at Comboni College, and they took me out to the village of Hella Mayo one Sunday when they were going to say Mass. A bongo drumbeat and applause greeted us upon our arrival. The mud-walled church building with a thatched roof was rudimentary, but the congregation was fervent. In addition to the spiritual work, the clergy was involved in the sponsorship of projects to dig a well and provide a water pump to get clean water for the community and build essential roads—basic infrastructure that made all the difference in the world to the village residents.

In Juba, the capital of southern Sudan (a now-independent nation that was then part of Sudan), the songs at Mass at St. Joseph's Church included "Michael, Row the Boat Ashore," the African American spiritual that had made its way into popular culture in the United States in the early 1960s. Hearing it sung in such a soulful and expressive way, on a hot, tropical African Sunday morning, made me nostalgic and a little homesick.

Kenya followed and was a land of austere beauty and fresh air, highlighted by a climb up Mount Kenya to Point Lenana (elevation 16,355 feet, or 4,985 meters), where a cross posted at the summit by the Consolata Fathers bore the inscription *"Christus Regnat"* (Christ Reigns). There were many drives and hikes through the spectacular countryside. In Nairobi, I watched President Daniel arap Moi deliver the Kenyatta Day speech, during which he freed 7,004 prisoners in honor of the occasion, and I visited the law courts, watching an appellate argument, a jury trial, and a bench (judge) trial. I also went to the Roman Catholic cathedral in Nairobi. It was full of light and life, with beautiful African music accompanying the Mass, celebrated by the papal nuncio (the pope's representative) in honor of the second anniversary of the papacy of John Paul II, making it a brilliant experience.

On a train through the Great Rift Valley, heading to Uganda, as I stood at an open window to view the passing scenery, people along the way evidently were watching me. Two young girls beside the tracks pointed to me and excitedly said, *"Muzungu"* (the Bantu/Swahili word for traveler), as they spotted me.

I went to Uganda because the border between Kenya and Tanzania was closed at the time, so a roundabout route was necessary to reach Kenya's southern neighbor. Shortly after I arrived, the forbearing temperament of the Ugandan people promptly revealed itself aboard a bus that went to Kampala, the capital, from the Kenyan border. It was around ten o'clock in the morning, and we were just a few miles north of the equator. The day was quickly becoming hot and humid as the bus filled with more and more people, becoming extremely overcrowded. There were many more passengers than there should have been, and it reached the point where, if a bad mood had gotten the better of someone, an ugly experience may have followed. But at just the right moment, when it seemed as if the circumstances had reached the limits of everyone's patience, several women started singing hymns. It completely broke the tension at just the right moment.

Like many of the countries through which I was traveling, Uganda used to be part of the British Commonwealth. Its legal system included English common law, which is also the root of the common law (law made by judges) in the United States. I was in an English-style courtroom in Kampala one day, with wigged judges in red robes and counsel in black robes. One of the Ugandan lawyers cited the case called *Hadley v. Baxendale*, a famous 1854 English decision we had studied in law school, which established the principle that a party who breaches a contract is liable for mutually foreseeable losses. The lawyer urged the court to apply *Hadley v. Baxendale* to the facts of his client's case. I do not remember the particular facts, but I do recall my excitement at the prospect of holding in common with fellow lawyers in Africa the same legal propositions that govern the breach of agreements in America.

Another milestone of my professional life occurred in Uganda at that same time. I had taken the Ohio bar examination that summer in July and was passing through the country when the results were supposed to become available. I had to call back home to get the score from the Supreme Court of Ohio. That was not easy. It required reserving an international phone line for an evening call to reach the Supreme Court during its normal business hours in Ohio, which were eight hours behind Uganda time. On the day I expected the results to be released, I reserved a phone line at a large local hotel. The call went through, but to my frustration, the results were not yet available.

It was dusk in Kampala as I walked casually back to my own hotel. People on the street started urging me to "hurry, hurry, go home fast." What I did not know but could clearly hear from the rooftop once I got back to my hotel was that gunfire commonly broke out on the streets at nightfall, and it was not safe. The government had been overthrown when dictator Idi Amin was forced out of power in April 1979. Kampala was still largely in ruins. The city was dotted with the rubble of buildings destroyed amid the fighting, and the infrastructure was patchy. The nighttime volleys should have been no surprise to me in that setting.

Thus forewarned, I headed back to my hotel more swiftly the next evening, after I again called back to Ohio, this time from the local post office. I had the benefit of an extra spring in my step on returning to my hotel that night. The person whom I reached at the Supreme Court of Ohio gave me the good news that I had passed the bar exam. It was a real relief, especially in view of the cramming I had to do in my self-study preparation. I looked forward to taking the oath of admission upon my return to Ohio so I could start my work as a lawyer.

On the Sunday morning before moving on, the Luganda-language Mass in Kampala was notable for the applause of the congregation at the consecrations of the sacramental bread and wine. After such an eventful time in Uganda, I went by boat across the gray waters of Lake Victoria to Bukoba, in Tanzania, and headed to Arusha, at the foot of Mount Kilimanjaro, intent on getting there before the rainy season.

Climbing Mount Kilimanjaro

Climbing Mount Kilimanjaro was, literally and figuratively, the high point of the trip. The mountain is approximately at the halfway mark between Cairo and Cape Town and presides over the Serengeti plains in a uniquely majestic way. The summit is the highest point in Africa, at 19,340 feet (5,895 meters), way above the clouds. The climb is an extended hike. No technical climbing equipment is necessary. Going up takes three and a half days, and then it is a day and a half to come down. Usually, the trek is made in groups, with a mandatory contingent of guides and porters. The team with which I climbed included ten Italian mountain climbers, who were a lot of fun, with terrific senses of humor and enviable agility.

The starting point is on the wooded grassland savanna of Tanzania, with dense foliage and lots of birds. We stayed in huts overnight on the way up. During our ascent, the trees and shrubs became increasingly sparse with the altitude. By the end, the hike took us across bare rock. The air grew progressively thinner on the way, with less and less oxygen content as we proceeded.

The first day of our ascent was Election Day in the United States—the presidential election of November 1980. I had cast an absentee ballot from the US embassy in Kampala in October. Of course, I was curious about who would win. This was before cell phones or Wi-Fi. My guide, Anasioni Mmbando, was able to keep abreast of the news by radio. At breakfast the next morning, he told me, "Reagan is the winner. The news from Dar es Salaam says it is by a big vote." That was a surprise to me because Governor Reagan had previously cast himself as an archconservative, and I had been away from the United States during the closing months of the campaign, when his charm won the votes of millions of Americans. One of the Italian climbers, who had an ability to find humor in any situation, spread his arms and proclaimed, "*Habemus presidente*" (We have a president), in the manner of the announcement of a new pope from the balcony of St. Peter's Basilica.

On the second evening, as we camped midway up the slopes of Mount Kilimanjaro, I listened with the guides and porters to the shortwave radio broadcast in Swahili, the official language of Tanzania and Kenya, from the Tanzanian capital. The announcer kept talking about "Bwana Reagan" (Lord Reagan), confirming that Ronald Reagan had won the White House from the incumbent president, Jimmy Carter. The guides and porters finished the evening memorably, singing Lutheran hymns along with the song "Kilimanjaro" and the African anthem "*Mungu ibariki Afrika*" ("God bless Africa") as we gazed out over the plains of Africa, over twelve thousand feet below us.

The final ascent was exhilarating. We all went to bed in a rustic hut on the third night at 5:45 p.m., when it was barely dusk, after a light and easily digestible meal of potato soup. The guides awakened us at 12:30 a.m. so we could reach the summit by sunrise. It was freezing that high up the mountain. Warm clothing was essential. I put on much of what I had brought to Africa: two pairs of pants, three pairs of socks, two T-shirts, one shirt, a sweater, and a pullover, plus a rented parka and boots.

The view was stunning when we stepped outside into the dark night. Above us, we could see the Milky Way, hundreds of constellations, and thousands of stars, including many falling stars. I wrote in the journal I kept on the trip that we were "guided by kerosene lanterns up the scree [loose stone] slope" and took "small steps and many stops," which we needed to catch our breath due to the diminishing oxygen content of the rarified air. Just before dawn, one of the planets appeared as a morning star above Mawenzi Peak (below us at 16,893 feet), and the "thin clouds above became brilliant red just before sunrise." We had some tea to keep warm, then headed up to Uhuru (Freedom) Peak.

We reached Uhuru Peak, the highest point in Africa, after an additional hour's climb, having stopped after every five steps for more oxygen. There we saw the sun rise over Africa, an utterly beautiful sight that gives anyone who sees it optimism sufficient to last a lifetime. We were literally on top of the world, at least that part of it, after a strenuous three-day climb. The simplicity, purity, and clarity of the moment were overwhelming. The summit was a glaciated "flat plateau, covered with shining white snow" at the time, and gave us all a "feeling of euphoria." Despite the cloud cover far below, from which the sun emerged over the eastern horizon, we were able to clearly see Mount Kenya about three hundred miles to the north. When the clouds parted, we could see the ground several miles below us.

Inside a wooden chest at the top of Uhuru Peak was a book climbers could sign. Next to my signature, I left the comment "Ain't No Mountain High Enough," the title of the Motown song that was the perfect expression of how I felt in the exuberance of that moment.

The way down would *seem* to be easy. The climber almost skis through thousands of feet of small pebbles due to the steep incline. In many ways, though, the descent was just as challenging as the trip up because it put prolonged pressure on rarely used muscles after the arduous work of the preceding days.

During the descent, English-speaking climbers on the way up filled me in on the US election details. I was disappointed to learn it had been a tough day across the board for Democrats, with key losses in the congressional elections as well. As a gauge of American influence around the world in that era, it was telling to meet a couple from Sweden who had delayed their departure for Africa several weeks so they could watch the US presidential candidate debates. A few days later, and many miles down the road, I was asked, "Do you think President Carter will give up the throne?" I assured the gentleman we always have peaceful transitions of power in America. Forty years later, if he heard the news from Washington on January 6, 2021, he may rightfully have wondered what had become of that tradition.

Traveling from Tanzania to Zambia

After coming down from Mount Kilimanjaro, I headed to Dar es Salaam, the capital of Tanzania, by overnight bus from Arusha. The bus broke down in the middle of the night (3:30 a.m.) on a rough road in a remote part of the grassland countryside. As we got off and were waiting for the repair work to be completed, we could hear a drumbeat in the distance. One of the other young passengers, who saw I was as interested in it as he was, said, "Let us go and collect ideas." We walked toward the sound of the drumbeat and ended up in a little village where a huge bonfire was crackling, encircled by a ring of people who were dancing, singing, and screeching. I can still hear the bongos and smell the woodsmoke of the village where we went to "collect ideas." The villagers welcomed us to stay, but before long, we had to get back to the bus before it left us behind.

One thing that made a big difference there and elsewhere in Africa in allowing me to engage with people was learning basic phrases in the local languages, including Arabic and Swahili. It was all fragmentary on my part—I could learn only a little—but it made such a difference. I found that people were open to developing some kind of relationship with me because I had taken the time to learn about them.

In Dar es Salaam, Sir Philip Biron of the Tanzanian high court welcomed me to his chambers, where we talked about double jeopardy, witchcraft, President Julius Nyerere, and human nature. An evening walk made another lasting impression. The presidential palace sat in arabesque splendor near the shore of the Indian Ocean. The grounds were full of peacocks. At dusk they made the most enchanting cooing sound. Decades later a talented sculptor in Columbus cast a life-size bronze peacock statue for me. It now graces our home and is named Julius, after President Nyerere, the national hero who was then in office.

I went from Tanzania to Zambia by the Tazara Railway, a new railroad that had opened five years earlier as a cooperative project of the governments of Tanzania, Zambia, and the People's Republic of China. Food seemed scarce along the way. In Zambia, it was interesting to meet with several business executives and lawyers and learn from them about the economic and legal challenges the landlocked nation faced.

Throughout the trip, the economic challenge I myself faced in stretching my limited funds proved to be a virtue. I had just two thousand dollars on which to live for four months but managed to find affordable accommodations. Beds were available on outdoor verandas at night for thirty-five cents (with a shower in the courtyard) or for slightly more at a youth hostel, so the money could be spread out. A good dinner in most villages cost fifty cents. The benefit of the low-budget approach is the daily opportunity, of necessity, to meet people eye to eye and have many person-to-person experiences.

Zimbabwe and Matusadona National Park

After leaving Lusaka, the Zambian capital, a series of car rides, boat trips, and a short plane flight took me to Lake Kariba, the largest man-made lake in the world, and Matusadona National Park in Zimbabwe. There I was introduced to the park warden named John Steven and his wife Nicci. A gentleman who had given me a ride from Lusaka was a friend of theirs and recommended I stay with them. At the time, Zimbabwe—which until recently had been called Rhodesia—was emerging from the colonial era of white-dominated government and had converted to majority rule a couple of months before.

When I arrived at Matusadona, a bushfire was raging. I had seen the smoke the night before from the place where I was staying several miles away. Everyone was called to action. John Steven pointed to me and said, in his park warden voice, "Leave your bags here and come with me. Get in the Land Rover." I went with him, and we made our way to the nearby laborers' village, where he collected twenty to thirty local men and several additional vehicles. We headed directly toward the fire, which was burning at three different sites, and reached it after a long walk up and down many hills.

John said to me, "Okay, you take those guys, and I'll take these guys. You go over there and get that part of the fire out." Everything happened too quickly for me to be frightened. All of a sudden, I was right in the middle of the bushfires. Everybody instinctively knew what to do as we methodically swatted the fires with branches from nearby trees, moving forward in a loose semblance of a line. Although it became difficult to see as it got dark, we managed to put out the fires unscathed.

I stayed at Matusadona for several days. In addition to letting me pick and eat all the fresh mangoes I wanted, John gave me a Jeep with a guide (who had a rifle for our protection) to go out all day onto the savanna, looking for wildlife to observe. We were perched far enough away that the animals would not sense our presence. It was wonderful—in the literal sense of the word—to watch a rhinoceros or a zebra walk past. One night John took me with him out into the bush, where the elephants knew him well enough that we could go right up to them. That was one of the moments that made me truly appreciate animals in the wild. When *they* choose to interact with *you*, it is amazing.

The unanticipated part of the trip was the love I developed for the wildlife of Africa. I went to Africa to learn about law and politics and meet judges with whom I could talk about their professional experiences. I ended up learning so much more. Because it was such a low-budget trip, I was ordinarily out in the countryside, living on the land the animals roamed. That became an awe-inspiring experience. When you look out onto the hillsides and plains, you can see elephants and giraffes and other creatures as they move freely through the bush and trees. It made me realize this is as much their world as it is ours.

Along the way from Cairo to Cape Town, I saw baboons, colorful birds of many sorts, buffalo, butterflies, camels, crested cranes, crocodiles, eagles, eland, elephant, gazelle, giraffe, guinea fowl, hippos, impala, kudu, mongoose, monkeys, peacocks, waterbuck, wildebeest, and zebra. I started to seek out encounters with animals as I traveled southward through Africa. When I got back to the United States, I applied to serve on the board of trustees of the Columbus Zoo. I had become so enamored by my firsthand experiences with animals that I wanted to continue them in whatever way possible and find a means to expose other people to them.

When I was making my way down the African continent, I did not give too much thought to my personal safety and, in retrospect, regret what I inadvertently put my parents through. Back then there were no GPS trackers and no cell phones with which to stay in touch. And going in, I was oblivious to the risks. On many days, I was hitchhiking, which was common then and there but not wise on many levels. But it was not just a matter of being snapped up by the wrong *person* like in the US—there could be leopards around . . . or lions, snakes, or any number of other wildlife dangers. When you realize that, you hope a car or truck will stop *soon*.

Apartheid South Africa

I reached South Africa in early December, crossing over from Zimbabwe at Beit Bridge. It was a warm and pleasant summer outdoors. Nearly every place was beautiful in its own way, from the mountains and hills on the way to Johannesburg, through the countryside and the Great Karoo desert, and on to the Stellenbosch region and Cape Town.

For me, as a traveler who had come to *learn*, though, the exceptional thing about my time in South Africa was it forced me to react—for the first time in my life—to unavoidable racial issues in a direct and practical way. The apartheid laws required segregation of almost everything by race—

there were strict rules about where people of Black African descent could be, where people of Indian descent could be, and where people of white European descent could be. It was extremely rigid. It occurred to me it was reminiscent of what the Southern United States must have looked like in the years before the Civil War as I passed large groups of Black agricultural laborers working crops in far-flung fields under the supervision of a rifle-carrying white overseer on horseback. I had not thought much beforehand about how to deal with the apartheid system. But the minute I crossed the border, it hit me. At that point, I had to decide.

I concluded the "best policy is to disregard apartheid system," as I noted at the time. I certainly did not want to support or cooperate with such a practice but also did not want to acknowledge its authority by basing my every movement on contradicting it. And, as a general rule, I vastly preferred to treat people as individuals rather than as members of a group. So I just ignored it. The situation presented itself, for example, when a Black funeral home driver with whom I had hitched a ride dropped me off at the "non-European" entrance (in the South African vernacular) to a train station. I went in that door instead of looking for the whites-only entrance. When I was waiting for trains, I would step into whichever car stopped in front of me on the platform, regardless of the race for which it was designated. Going into a grocery store, a chain-link fence would sometimes divide the entrance between one side for whites and the other for nonwhites. I would use whichever side was closer, drawing gasps on one occasion from two young Black girls as I entered on their side of the fence.

In retrospect, I think I avoided arrest in South Africa because people probably thought I was just another judgmental American. I remember one man saying to me sardonically, "We wake up every morning here and listen to the radio to hear what the United States wants us to do today." It was during the Carter administration, and the US was taking more of an initiative against apartheid. I found that ignoring the racial restrictions gave me a color-blind exposure to the local way of life—which I wanted to see—without submitting to such a peculiar system.

Only when I went to a government office in Johannesburg to get a pass to go to Soweto, the largest Black township in South Africa, did I encounter any resistance. The desk officer declined to issue the permit, on the grounds "it is too dangerous" and "you will probably be killed there." An attorney intervened at my request with the officer's supervisor, who reluctantly granted the necessary pass. Once I got to Soweto, I did not sense any unusual jeopardy and found instead a bleak but hospitable community.

While I was in Cape Town, I became friends with a journalist for *The Argus*, and he and his wife let me stay with them. His work was quite interesting because he was part of the English-speaking journalism community, which tended to be more liberal, more critical of apartheid, and less sympathetic to the white Afrikaner population. To see South Africa through their eyes gave me a much more rounded perspective on the untenable situation, which collapsed fourteen years later.

South Africa was my final stop. I was in Cape Town just before Christmas in December, at the height of the African summer. The city was picturesque, with warm sunshine beating down and palm trees swaying in the breeze. Close to the southern tip of the continent, the Indian Ocean on one side meets the Atlantic Ocean on the other. On my final day, on the first leg of the flight home, to Rio de Janeiro, several passengers (Brazilians returning from Mozambique) brought out drums and other musical instruments once we reached cruising altitude and started playing them for quite some time. I changed planes in Rio de Janeiro, then flew on to New York and Columbus. We landed at JFK Airport on a cold and gray winter morning, evidenced by the frosty breath of the ground attendants as they motioned the plane to the gate. I knew the trip was over.

Embracing Differences That Better Define Us

I had noticed in law school that my classmates who had gotten exposure to the world through travel seemed to have special insight—a deeper way of looking at life. That encouraged me to travel then and has continued to motivate me ever since. Maryline and I have traveled a lot and taken our son and daughter along with us since they were babies, instilling a love of adventure in them too. It is a blessing we have been determined to pass on.

Immersion in such different cultures as I encountered in Africa made me more resolute about my own identity. Rather than fear or belittle differences that might threaten me, I learned to embrace them because they actually had the opposite effect. They allowed me to see more clearly who I am by comparison and what I might be able to contribute to the world. I left Africa not so much transformed as inspired to make the most of my own unique attributes and opportunities.

For me, at the time, Africa was a hugely important place at a hugely important turning point in my life. It is a unique part of the world. The many different people have a distinctive sense of self-possession and pride and are extraordinarily willing to share. It is also a beautiful place. The outdoors there is unlike anywhere else in the world, and I was outside most of the time by virtue of my low budget, means of travel, and rudimentary accommodations. In all respects, it was wonderful to be there.

The trip itself was an ideal way to absorb the experiences of my first twenty-six years. It gave me a transition between my formal education and the start of my professional life. After such an intense period of study, it was good to take a significant break before moving on to the next phase— and my good fortune to be able to do so. It was good for my head because I was in such a completely different environment for so long it cleared my mind and allowed me to refocus my thinking. I saw things from a different perspective from that distance. The accumulated experiences of many years settled in and set me up to start again with fresh enthusiasm. By the time I left Cape Town, I had not worked for over four months and was ready to come back and get on with being a lawyer.

Chapter 6:
Attorney at Law

It was time to make a decision about my professional future before I left for Africa. I had completed law school plus three law firm internships and a judicial clerkship. Those experiences had helped me to focus on the type of law in which I thought I could make the most use of whatever abilities I had.

Law Firm Clerkships

The process of finding law firm internships during law school had been new to me. In deciding where to apply, my classmates and I gathered information by word of mouth from students in classes ahead of us or from the Martindale–Hubbell directory or general reputation—the main ways of getting meaningful information in the pre-internet era. The firms that were interested in hiring ordinarily sent a lawyer to the law school. An on-campus interview lasting fifteen or twenty minutes followed for students who signed up. The firms then decided, based on that session, which students to invite to their offices for further interviews. We did not have standard grades, so there was no class rank for the firms to use as a metric. As students, we in turn were sizing up the law firms. There was always an element of stress, but the meetings were generally informative, and it was a great opportunity to learn. It was usually obvious who had interviews on any given day; we lived mostly in casual clothes at law school, so classmates who were dressed up stood out.

I was primarily interested in practicing law in Columbus, so I looked for opportunities locally the first summer. One of the largest law firms in Columbus was Porter Wright Morris & Arthur. The firm was kind enough to offer me a job as a first-year student, which I very much appreciated. I was lucky to get the position, as it was rare at the time for law firms to hire first-year law students during the summer. There were excellent lawyers at the Porter firm, and they had a comprehensive summer program. It was fun to work with summer associates from other schools. I took the work seriously. It was my first time drafting briefs and pleadings for actual clients. In addition to legal research, I prepared draft appellate briefs and motions for use in civil litigation (generally, cases between private parties). I liked the firm and the work and was fortunate to receive a job offer afterward.

In the second summer, I wanted to try working in New York as an alternative to coming back to Columbus. The better I understood the American economy and how it functioned, the more I wanted to see firsthand how it worked at its legal epicenter, which Wall Street seemed to be. Among the Wall Street law firms, Simpson Thacher & Barlett was one of the best, with a roster of highly distinguished lawyers. When the firm offered me a summer job, I accepted.

Students ahead of me who had worked there told me Simpson Thacher is "an excellent law firm, but there's one guy you don't want to have to work for because he's really tough and demanding." And so, on my first day, I got there and went through the orientation. The summer program administrator then picked me up and said, "Well, let's take you to your first assignment." And, of course, it was with that "one guy," Richard M. Dicke. It turned out to be a real bonus to work with Mr. Dicke, tough and demanding as he was. He was one of the leading lawyers for the electric utility industry in the United States. To me, he seemed to be the epitome of a lawyer in private practice. When I was waiting to talk with him about the progress on my assignment, I would sit in his office and listen to his phone conversations, giving me a glimpse of how he did business. It was enlightening to see how his comprehensive overview of the electric utility industry served him well in giving advice and counsel and advocating for his clients' needs.

The firm had an impressive office overlooking Battery Park in the Wall Street area. From the panoramic windows, I could look out and see the

Statue of Liberty and the Ellis Island immigration center. At the time, it had been a little over sixty years since my paternal grandparents had come through there. It was awesome to scan the harbor and wonder what they would have thought. My work there went well, and the firm offered me a job after my law school graduation.

The third and final summer opportunity came between graduation and the start of my judicial clerkship in August 1979. Jones, Day, Reavis & Pogue, a firm then based in Cleveland, was hiring, and I was fortunate to receive a summer job there and then a full-time job offer. The work involved a steady flow of legal research and writing on several significant litigation issues. In the process of interviewing with Jones Day, I met one of its partners, Oliver C. "Pudge" Henkel, who later would have a great impact on my career and who, despite his nickname, was one of the most athletic and outgoing individuals I had ever met.

It was also by virtue of that job that I had a memorable experience with the Olivet Institutional Baptist Church, a Black church on the east side of Cleveland. Its pastor, Reverend Dr. Otis Moss Jr., was one of the American leaders to whom President Jimmy Carter had publicly turned for advice on national affairs that summer. I was interested in hearing him and going to a Sunday service at a Black Baptist church. I called ahead one weekday to confirm the time and then hemmed and hawed a bit before telling the receptionist I was white and asking if it would be okay to attend. She paused for a moment and then said with great empathy, "Honey, this is God's house. Everyone is welcome here." Thus guided, I went and was glad to have gone.

The law firm internships taught me how to work in a law firm environment—which is different from other office settings—and gave me a better appreciation of what clients need from their lawyers. They helped me understand things to look for at a law firm: the types of people, the clients, the work, and the resources. In a summer program, law students are exposed to the different types of work a firm does. That can include projects ranging from litigation to tax work, corporate matters, employment issues, trust and estate proceedings, and a wide range of other subjects. The students can see what the firm's practice is like, its character, personality, standards, and expectations. Equally important is understanding *who* the firm's clients are and how people at the firm treat each other. And, of course, the law firm wants to evaluate the law student.

One of the key things I learned was that I naturally gravitated to the litigation practice and its various stages of discovery (fact-finding), legal research, writing, and oral argument. The career inspiration from those experiences was invaluable.

Clerking for Judge Gilbert S. Merritt Jr.

A judicial clerkship followed law school and my last summer job. The role of an appellate law clerk is to assist the judge in studying the record, analyzing the controlling cases and legal arguments, and drafting the opinion. Judge Gilbert S. Merritt Jr. of the United States Court of Appeals for the Sixth Circuit had posted a note on the job board at Yale Law School, saying he was a new federal judge appointed by President Jimmy Carter, had been an undergraduate at Yale, and was interested in talking with potential law clerks. I did some research and, drawn by what I learned about his background, applied and flew to Nashville, where he lived and had his judicial chambers, to meet for an interview.

We talked a lot about the philosopher John Rawls, whose book *A Theory of Justice* we both had read and greatly admired, and about Southern politics. Judge Merritt had previously served as United States Attorney for the Middle District of Tennessee and had spent several years before and after that in private practice. He was an extraordinarily bright man with a penetrating intellect and a knack for figuring out the key point of every case, the one fact or proposition of law on which the matter ultimately turned. I wanted to see how he did that and learn what I could about the practical application of the law.

The judicial clerkship was a one-year position, starting in August 1979. The court met in Cincinnati and reviewed decisions of federal trial courts in Kentucky, Michigan, Ohio, and Tennessee. Judge Merritt liked to probe and argue with his law clerks in his quest to find the key fact or law that decided the case. His two other law clerks (including my law school classmate Gary Tepper) and I lived in Nashville and traveled back and forth in shifts to Cincinnati for the oral argument sessions. Judge Merritt frequently flew his own small plane to and from home and the court. His longtime assistant Sara Pettit, also a law school graduate, deftly managed the judicial chambers in Nashville and Cincinnati and all of us who worked there.

The year with Judge Merritt also was an opportunity for immersion in Southern civic and political culture. Before going onto the bench, Judge Merritt had played an integral role in Tennessee politics on the Democratic side. The state of Tennessee was blessed with a number of distinctive political leaders from both major parties (including both generations of the Albert Gore family, senior and junior; Senator Howard Baker; and Governor Lamar Alexander). It appeared to me the civic leaders in Nashville had exerted a subtle but forceful influence that constructively guided the community through the civil rights movement of the postwar era. Their work had created an environment for peaceful, if gradual, progress. One of those leaders, John L. Seigenthaler, was a close friend of Judge Merritt. He was the longtime editor and publisher of the leading local newspaper, *The Tennessean*, and had been a Justice Department official in the Kennedy administration.

My impression at the time was that race relations were evolving in a more stable way in the South, where the races had coexisted for several centuries, than in the North, where the great migrations of the twentieth century had created new conditions to which all people were still adjusting.

A less tolerant welcome awaited the flood of Cuban refugees from the Mariel boatlift in the spring of 1980. When President Fidel Castro suddenly lifted restrictions on emigration in April 1980, thousands of Cubans began to arrive by boat in southern Florida. Many were taken to temporary housing at Eglin Air Force Base in the Florida Panhandle. A friend and I were in the vicinity at the time, on a weekend trip. During our afternoon visit to the air force base encampment, a small plane flew overhead with a trailing banner that said "Cubans Go Home." The message provoked concern among several hundred refugees gathered below at an outdoor meeting. It seemed to reassure the newcomers, though, when one of the military officers told them, "Don't worry about it. In America we have something in our Constitution called the First Amendment, and it lets people say whatever they want to say. You'll be okay."

We heard from a reporter that there was going to be a Ku Klux Klan rally in a field down the road that evening. We made plans to see it. The meeting was already underway when we arrived near dusk. We found an inconspicuous place far in the back. Assembled before us were hundreds of people garbed in the white robes and hoods for which the Klan is known. It was startling to see that sight with our own eyes. It was even more startling to see the people who were there in plainclothes; they looked just like everyone else we ordinarily saw on the street in day-to-day life. A large wooden cross had been staked in the ground. The main speaker was David Duke, Grand Wizard of the Klan. At the climax of his inflammatory remarks, the crowd took lit torches to the cross and set it afire. We recoiled, moving back even farther, and I stood on a small mound. Unbeknownst to me, it was a red ant hill. The ants began crawling up my legs and biting me as the flaming cross and burning torches lit up the night sky. Someone in the crowd spotted a passing car with open windows and yelled, "There's a bunch of n*****s. Let's get 'em." The Klansmen surged toward the road as the car sped away. We quickly headed out in the other direction. I had to rethink my conclusion about the comparative status of race relations in the South and North.

Going Back to Ohio

When I was deciding after law school where to work after the clerkship, people would ask me, "What is it about Ohio? Why not stay in New York?" I am sure I would have had a fulfilling experience if I had accepted the job offer on Wall Street. The work would have been fascinating and important, and New York is a vibrant international hub and center of the American economy. But I did not see a long-term future for myself in the city. By contrast, I could envision a lifetime of service and leadership in Ohio, where I had loved growing up, and a greater opportunity to put myself in challenging positions. Before I left Nashville, I lined up what turned out to be my long-term job, and after the journey through Africa, I returned to Ohio to start my legal career.

When I was growing up in Columbus, the law firm of Vorys, Sater, Seymour and Pease was the preeminent firm in town. It was founded in 1909 by the four namesake lawyers, three days before William Howard Taft of Ohio took the oath of office as president of the United States. The four partners soon afterward moved their offices to the third floor of a small building they opened in downtown Columbus, which the firm now fully occupies along with the neighboring buildings it gradually annexed over the intervening years. A bust of President (later Chief Justice) Taft overlooks the lobby, in continued recognition of his relationship with the founders. By the late 1970s the firm had grown to over 100 lawyers in the Columbus office. Today the firm includes over 375 attorneys practicing in ten offices in Ohio; Washington, DC; Texas; Pennsylvania; California; London; and Berlin. I looked at the firm with a touch of awe because of its reputation.

The first person from the firm I encountered was the gentleman who ran its copying machines. We met one Sunday at Mass at the St. Thomas More Newman Center when I was in college at Ohio State. His association with the firm impressed me, and I was excited to get to know him.

In addition to being impressed by the quality of the firm's work and lawyers and staff, it struck me that an unusually large number of people at the firm were involved in community leadership roles. Also important to me, having gotten a sense of what a big world it is, was a unique aspect of the firm called the Seymour Plan—a trust funded by James O. Seymour, a partner and son of one of the founders, that paid the round-trip airfare for several associates and staff members and their spouses every year to their farthest destination in Europe. Along with the Partners in Paris trust fund, which Mr. Seymour also established, the Seymour Plan infused the classic Midwestern firm with an unusually international and engaged outlook on the world.

After a round of job interviews, I accepted the job offer in a face-to-face conversation with James P. Kennedy, an antitrust lawyer who was then the head of the hiring committee, one day when he was in Cincinnati for an oral argument at the Sixth Circuit while I was there on other cases with Judge Merritt. As I saw even more clearly in the years that followed, Jim Kennedy had an uncanny ability to sum things up in a concise and convincing way. He also had a sound philosophy about life, which one of his sons shared in a eulogy at his funeral several decades later. "My dad had a sign at home," he said, "and it has three lines on it. The first line says 'Do it.' The second line says 'Do it right.' The third line says 'Do it right now.'" I admired Jim Kennedy even more after I heard that creed. Time is such a precious element. There are always reasons not to do things. Inertia is a powerful influence in all our lives. But diligent acts of will are almost always worth it because if you wait too long or do something in a careless way, the opportunity may be lost altogether.

Practicing Law at Vorys, Sater, Seymour and Pease

When I started on January 5, 1981, I had just flown in from Cape Town in late December, trading the warm, sunny African summer for the cold, gray Ohio winter. It had been beautiful at the southern tip of Africa—blue skies and ocean water, fresh air, and palm trees. I had been living a blissful existence there, and all of a sudden, it was a frigid January day in Ohio, and I was out of money, slipping and sliding on the ice to get to work.

Uncertain whether I had made the right choice by coming home, one thing that helped me adjust was a conversation I had with a college roommate. He said, "Don't think about it as going home. Think about it as going to a new place you're discovering." That clicked for me; I was able to view home with new eyes. It helped me to appreciate that it sometimes becomes a lot easier to adjust if you go into a familiar situation with fresh eyes and an open mind. It also helped that I quickly became completely immersed in the work assigned to me as a new associate in the firm's Litigation Group.

My first mentors at the firm were John Elam and David Cupps. John Elam was the presiding partner. He was a born leader and extraordinary trial lawyer. I was fortunate to be able to work on many cases with him in my early years at the firm. David Cupps was brilliant, articulate, outrageously funny, and hardworking. He would be in the office sometimes until two thirty in the morning, as I know because I was there too until we finished what we were doing. He was a consummate lawyer. I learned so much from the two of them. Being on cases with each of them was the best immersion for which I could have hoped. The hours were long, and I was constantly adapting to different circumstances, but I was able to adjust.

Generally, I started at seven thirty in the morning and was so focused on the work that—before I knew it—it was dinner time. I would usually get something from a fast-food restaurant or call for pizza delivery, then keep on working. Many of my early cases involved coordination with out-of-town counsel, mostly from New York. They had high demands and expectations and kept similar hours. From morning to night, the work involved research and writing, along with occasional court appearances for trials or hearings on motions. I usually caught the last bus home. It went on like that, day after day. I was single with no children or other responsibilities, so I did not have to be home at a certain time, and stamina has never been an issue.

What was important to remember throughout that grind was that it is good to be busy, and in a law firm you do not want to be under-occupied. If you are doing good work, clients and colleagues will keep coming to you as long as you have the capacity for it. If they see you have capacity, they will ask you to do more. I needed to learn to say no sometimes. The big difference between working all-nighters as a student and working in a law firm is that as a student, you know the term is going to wrap up and there will be a break, but at a law firm, when one case closes, the next one comes along, and . . . it never ends.

I quickly observed that—regardless of how busy I was—it is vitally important to take every project seriously. You cannot afford to overlook the small things. As an associate, I was doing the work to free up the partner so they could focus on other aspects of the case. If they had to redo work I was handing them, it would have been a colossal waste of my time *and* theirs. So, do it right the first time, regardless of how mundane it sometimes seems. When I did that, I found that good work begets more work. People gain confidence in you, and you are asked to join teams of other lawyers who are all determined to get the job done well on other cases.

My caseload, beginning with that first year, was quite varied. Some cases involved corporate mergers and acquisitions—reorganizations on a large scale. That meant they were important financially to the clients, with millions of dollars at stake. By one count, the firm was involved in twenty-five out of twenty-nine corporate takeovers in Ohio in the early 1980s. Other cases were on the opposite end of the financial spectrum but no less important to the people involved. Each client deserved the law firm's best efforts.

One week I accompanied John Elam to the United States Court of Appeals for the Sixth Circuit on a huge corporate takeover case he was arguing on behalf of one of the world's largest oil corporations. The case had high financial stakes for the client and was a major engagement at our firm. The following week I was back by myself in the same court on a pro bono case (legal work without charge) the court had asked me to argue for a prisoner—a man who had been convicted of murder. He was in one of the Ohio penitentiaries and was seeking a writ of habeas corpus (the writ Justice Wilson Arymaba had extolled so fervently during our conversation in Sudan) so the federal court could determine whether his conviction by the state court was lawful. One of the three judges on the panel for that appeal, Judge Bailey Brown, had also sat on the corporate takeover panel the week before. As I argued, he cut in to say—in his mellifluous Memphis accent—"I just want everybody to know that Mr. Kulewicz was here last week on a huge corporate takeover case, and now he's here as pro bono counsel for this prisoner. I think that's mighty fine and distinguished."

My imprisoned client and I did not manage to prevail in the appeal, but I took to heart the message I heard between the lines of Judge Brown's gracious praise. In every case, the lawyer's job is to assist the court in reaching the right conclusion regardless of the status of the parties. Good judges want to get it right.

I had gotten a foreshadowing of that sentiment as I walked into the courthouse that morning, when one of the other judges on that panel, Judge Boyce F. Martin Jr., stopped me in the lobby. He motioned me over and said, "Mr. Kulewicz, I just want to tell you your brief was so good. Thank you." It meant a lot to hear that from Judge Martin, who already had taught me a good lesson by example in an earlier case. He was one of the younger and more liberal members of the court. On one occasion the year before, when I was a law clerk for Judge Merritt, he was on a panel with one of the most conservative members of the court, an elderly judge. As the two of them and the third judge came out onto the bench for that oral argument, I watched with naive wonder as Judge Martin was kind enough to pull back and hold the chair for his older, conservative colleague. It was instructive to see such innate common courtesy between judges who could not have been further apart in terms of their judicial philosophies.

Officer of the Court

My experience on the day of the habeas corpus oral argument was the first of many times I learned the lesson that a lawyer's job is to be an officer of the court as well as a zealous advocate for the client. The lawyer, like the judge, must promote justice and serve the system for everyone involved in the process. As an officer of the court, the lawyer's main job is not only to represent the client vigorously but also to assist the judge or jury in reaching the right conclusion. Thinking of the lawyer's role that way is simply an adaptation of the adage "always think of the next person," which has led at least one international automobile manufacturer to great success. By presenting a well-prepared witness or delivering a well-informed argument, the lawyer provides the necessary ingredients to make a sound decision. When a judge and jury see that the lawyer is facilitating their work and providing what they need to reach the correct result, they become engaged. And that is a rewarding moment.

Virtually every judge with whom I have ever dealt has wanted to do the job right as they see it. That is their responsibility, and they take the role seriously. When they understand that I am trying to help them, even while my objective is for my client to win, it creates a more conducive environment. They become more amenable to considering the pros and cons of the argument being presented. To win, it is still imperative to be convincing, of course, but it is essential to share the process as a collaborative effort, supplementing their knowledge with facts and logic.

Conversely, if judges think the lawyer is distracting them or wasting their time—which is the worst-case scenario—things break down quickly. I have seen many judges bristle at opposing counsel who go down inadvisable paths. Fortunately, I have not been on the receiving end all that often. Judges almost universally condemn lawyers for bickering over personal issues. Such lawyers end up defeating themselves. The judges regard it as a total waste of time and prefer to focus on the merits of the case.

Each judge's perception of fairness is fundamental to what they regard as important. It can be influenced by many factors, such as their views of history and expectations of your work quality. The lawyer must adapt accordingly. The impression the lawyer should aim to give *every* judge—even if they have never met before—is of someone who is completely straightforward, respectful of the judge's role, diligent in getting things right, and willing to engage in a constructive back-and-forth about the case. While representing a client, the lawyer needs to be realistic about the strengths and weaknesses of the case. A lawyer probably cannot win every single case but *can* always give his or her best.

Protecting Our Clients

My practice has spanned a wide range of civil matters and kept me fully occupied for forty-four years. The engagements have included everything from state government procurement to professional boxing—and how natural gas pipelines work, how the state lottery functions, how petroleum companies explore and drill for oil and natural gas, how coal mining operates, how the secondary lending market works, liquor control and regulation, family trusts, credit ratings of financial instruments, law enforcement operations, collective bargaining, mayoral recalls, election law, professional licensing and placement, construction, commercial lending, accounting and auditing, philanthropic giving, discontinuance of law partnerships, class actions, adult and child guardianships, journalistic freedom of expression, defamation, foreign corrupt payment investigations, and many other subjects.

I have had the opportunity to protect and help people in a wide range of circumstances. Every case boils down to the people involved and what they are up against. Protecting people is what I love most about the lawyer's role in the legal process. When a big company is the client, the lawyer must gain an understanding of who the decision-maker is, what the company's culture is, what the company expects from the lawyer, and what the company hopes to achieve. Getting that right involves a lot of time, insight, and work. When the client is an individual, it is equally important to know and understand that person to effectively protect them.

Over the years, some of the most professionally satisfactory cases have been similar. There are oral arguments either in the court of appeals or trial court, and they are set for a short amount of time, but if the case is unusually significant and the judges—and the lawyers—are well prepared, they end up going on for an extended duration. In those circumstances the lawyers can fully flesh out the case, talk about everything that is of interest to the judge, and have a completely adequate opportunity to make their clients' points.

In one such case the closing arguments had been set for just thirty minutes per side. But the judge was so good, and all the lawyers were so well prepared, that the closing arguments ended up going for several hours. There was a considerable amount of back-and-forth with the judge and the other counsel, and it was extremely productive. The judge had done thorough homework, giving rise to excellent questions, and we were well prepared. When he delivered his opinion several weeks later, he closed it out with a paragraph that was complimentary of the efforts of counsel.

One other lesson I learned early in my career is that the lawyer must try to help other people understand what the lawyer understands, and that can result in a collaborative outcome. By nature litigation is an adversarial process, especially if there are good lawyers on both sides. The lawyers must be direct about the evidence—here is my client's set of facts, and here is the other person's set of facts—but if it is done right, it all helps the decision-maker. When you are dealing with facts, the temptation is sometimes to ignore the inconvenient ones. I would never misstate a fact, and I learned quickly that things you ignore rapidly come back to bite you. You are better off facing up to them.

I soon also learned that no two cases are alike; every case is new. The lawyer has to understand what the facts are and how the legal argument fits together so that when the judge asks questions, they can respond with authority and point the judge in the right direction.

The cases I found to be the most engaging were those in which the subject matter was new to me. That required a lot of learning, starting from the basics to grasp the intricacies involved. Such an exercise is instrumental to success, as it mirrors the process most judges undergo. Judges, despite their normally vast experience, frequently encounter situations that are unfamiliar to them, requiring them to learn the particular facts and the applicable law. Consequently, a crucial aspect of a lawyer's role is to understand what and how we have learned about a case. Such an understanding enables a lawyer to present the case to the judge succinctly and effectively, getting to the crux of the matter. The facts are of utmost importance. As a veteran federal appellate court judge once observed to me, the law stays pretty much the same over the years, and it is the facts that make each case interesting.

People normally reach out to litigators when they need help—when something has gone wrong in their lives or someone has sued them. I began to appreciate how satisfactory it is to provide that help after I started working with clients. Once you start dealing with clients, you can see it is real people with whom you are walking out of court, with their lives changed in one way or another as a result of what you have or have not been able to do. It is a huge responsibility. And that responsibility never leaves you. The lawyer must understand and protect the client.

Amid one of my first cases, we were just reaching a settlement agreement. The client looked at me point-blank and asked, "What do you think I should do?" For a young lawyer, it was a daunting moment. But that is what clients really want from a lawyer. They need considered advice about what to do in difficult situations. The lawyer must be comfortable giving that advice and defending the client's interests.

My responsibilities grew over time. Throughout the first few years, I worked as an associate on a combination of larger and smaller cases. I became a partner on January 1, 1987. Thirty-five years later, with a team of talented and dedicated colleagues, I was able to argue and win a case in the Supreme Court of the United States that made life better for 157 million Americans. Each case was equally important to the people involved. For a couple with modest means, determining whether they have a life estate in certain property is as crucial as a nearly billion-dollar tax liability is in another case to the taxpayer and public entity it concerns. By the time a case goes to court, it has to be pretty important to the client, as they are going to have to spend a lot of time—and money—on it.

Reckoning with the Situation

People, including me, who aspire in their youth to become lawyers often imagine only being in the courtroom, presenting arguments to a judge or jury. That is certainly the highlight of the litigation practice. It was only when I gained experience in the legal profession that I realized the bulk of the work would be understanding people, their culture, and their expectations.

I strive to do my best, and that begins with hard work behind the scenes—finding the relevant evidence and bringing in the best people. For instance, there have been times when expert witnesses presented testimony in court. When they and I have done our jobs well, the evidence becomes highly effective. In several cases the experts were so well prepared that the courtroom fell silent during their direct examinations and cross-examinations. Everyone put down their papers to listen intently, knowing something important was being said. When the judge picks up a pen to take notes, you know the examination is making a difference, helping the judge or jury understand the case better. That makes it all worthwhile.

Of course, not every case goes your way. There have been many times when I woke up in the middle of the night, suddenly realizing the significance of a fact or simply feeling the acute difficulty of the situation. It is painful but presents the need to accept the situation and find a way to deal with it. The best approach is to make a game plan for addressing the issue. If other options are exhausted, and it becomes clear the case is going to end unfavorably, the lawyer still must keep fighting until the end. At that point, it becomes a matter of damage control.

It is personally challenging when this happens. It is the client's case, but as their representative, I constantly ask myself, *Could I do this better? Is there something different we could do to change the outcome?* I keep reexamining the client's position to evaluate whether I am doing my best. Persistence helps; I just keep going. Sometimes there is an impasse—not a conflict of interest, because in those situations we do not take the case, but an argument with which the lawyer is uncomfortable. In those situations I have tried to figure out why I am feeling that way because if I am, the judge—or the decision-maker, the jury, or other individual or body—may be uncomfortable with it too.

There has never been a time when I have advocated for a client or an issue in which I did not believe. However, there are sometimes complexities in a case, and you can see there are genuinely two sides to the story. In that situation, you figure out both sides and what the ideal resolution would be while maximizing your client's position (how to "domesticate the intractable reality," in the immortal words of Professor Ackerman). These are often the cases that settle. Settling a case is something generally learned from experience and from watching more senior lawyers.

One advantage of working in the same jurisdiction for so long is you get to know a lot of the people involved in the process. With opposing counsel, by this stage, I have had several cases with or against most of them, so we have become increasingly acquainted with each other. With any luck, we can size up situations quickly and get to a result faster than if we did not know and respect each other. Once you know people, even if they are on the other side, you can have much more productive encounters.

Mentors

I have learned something from everyone with whom I have worked at the law firm, as well as from the clients, judges, court personnel, and opposing counsel who have been involved in the cases I have handled. What I learned from my early mentors, John Elam and David Cupps, was characteristic of what I learned from others.

John Elam joined the firm in 1949 when there were just 10 lawyers. By the time I got there in 1981, there were 125 lawyers, and he was the presiding partner. During his tenure that number grew to over 200 lawyers in multiple cities, and he was a pathbreaker along the way. John and the firm were proud to support trailblazers, including the first female associate at a large Columbus law firm, one of the first female partners at a Midwestern law firm, and the first African American partner at the firm. John's leadership ability was inspirational. With a strong dose of self-confidence, complete commitment to the firm and its clients, and sound judgment about getting to the bottom of things, he instinctively managed a large team of talented and strong-minded lawyers, ultimately to the benefit of the clients whom we served.

He was always direct and had an instinctive knack for talking to judges. Over the years I watched him and learned a lot. John would always get to the key facts and issues of a case and hammer on them. He also believed in transparency and getting ahead of an issue. His view was that if there is something bad out there, account for it and get ahead of it. It was always of utmost importance to John to be zealous in pursuit of the client's interest and candid with the courts. As he showed me time after time, it is important to be straight with judges. And, as a result, he was highly regarded by both the federal and state judiciaries in Ohio. When he retired, the local federal judges invited him to the courthouse for a luncheon in his honor because he had established such credibility with them. He was utterly professional, which was a great thing for me to see at such an early age.

John and I traveled together several times, during which he encouraged my interest in the use of foreign languages for the benefit of our clients. When we were in Japan for a case once, he overheard me speaking a few phrases in Japanese. I had learned enough of the language before visiting to be minimally conversational. On the way to Japan, we had stopped in Los Angeles and had a meal with one of John's friends from a local law firm. The friend told John his firm had an associate who had learned Japanese, and their practice really took off as a result. After John overheard me in Tokyo, he said, "When we get back to Columbus, I want you to enroll in the Japanese courses at Ohio State." I did so and ultimately took four quarters of Japanese, which provided a basic grasp of the language. It was a fun, if challenging, language to study and proved to be modestly helpful on occasion in supporting the work of the many Japan-based businesses the firm was already honored to represent.

Years later, when my family and I went to Japan, my limited ability to speak Japanese was useful in finding our way—and a source of amusement not only to my family but also to the Japanese people with whom I sought to talk. The conversations mainly had to do with matters such as finding the train to Kyoto or the bus to Mount Fuji. Along with the unintended entertainment value, these conversations also showed the benefit of learning to speak with people in their own language.

For a trip to Moscow in 1985, I learned enough Russian to make a presentation to the appropriate official in the Ministry of Sport on behalf of Columbus native Jerry Page, who had won a gold medal for the United States at the 1984 Olympics. The Soviet Union had boycotted the 1984 games in Los Angeles in retaliation for the US boycott of the 1980 Olympics in Moscow. We proposed to set up a match between my client and his Russian counterpart. The presentation went well, but the Soviets remained intransigent, and the match never took place.

My client Jerry Page (the 1984 Olympic gold medal boxer) and I pose for a photo. (Reproduced with permission from Columbus Citizen, Grandview Heights Public Library, *Columbus Citizen-Journal and* Columbus Citizen *Newspapers Collection.)*

A family sabbatical in Paris in 1991 provided an opportunity to improve upon my limited ability to speak, read, and write French, the foreign language I had taken as an undergraduate. The law firm had a sabbatical program that allowed partners to take three months off at certain intervals. Maryline and I rented an apartment in the Paris suburb of Neuilly-sur-Seine and lived there with Adam (before Abigail was born). Up to then my limited undergraduate French proficiency had come in handy only once, in my capacity as a member of the board of trustees of the Columbus Zoo. I had drafted correspondence to several French-speaking government officials in western Africa for the purpose of finding a female forest elephant to bring to the Columbus Zoo as a mate for our lonely male forest elephant. Quite specialized vocabulary was needed in that instance.

Our three-month sabbatical in Paris was an ongoing opportunity to use the language for general purposes every day (buying a television, opening a bank account, and so on). The next year I successfully took the examination of the Paris Chamber of Commerce for the *Certificat pratique de français commercial et economique.* Maryline, who is from France, subsequently spent a summer at Middlebury College in its intensive French training program, picking back up the language she had spoken as a child before coming to the United States.

John Elam helped me become the lawyer I am now, even outside the courtroom. One night, he and I were scheduled to fly to New York City for a case. Earlier that same day, John had been talking with the head of a bank in Columbus and mentioned we would be going to New York later that evening. By coincidence, the bank had chartered a private plane to fly former Secretary of State Henry A. Kissinger, who was its guest in Columbus that day, back to New York. John's banker friend said we would be welcome to travel with him.

It was the night of the United Nations Security Council vote in November 1990 on whether to go to war in Kuwait—the Desert Storm initiative in 1991. We spent a great deal of the in-flight time talking about the fast pace of the serious developments in the Middle East. As the junior member of the traveling party, it became my job to hold and equitably apportion the peanuts and other hors d'oeuvres while we talked—and absorb as much as I could from the conversation between two consummate masters of their respective professions.

The lessons I learned from John, a born competitor, helped me immeasurably in later heading up teams of colleagues on large-scale cases and pursuing the objectives of our clients. In putting teams together, I have made it a priority to find people who know more than me, to invest them with substantial responsibility, to listen to them, to understand their perspectives, to be direct about our goals, and to be thoroughly involved in the case myself. The results have been excellent.

John also taught me about settling cases. When I first started practicing, I assumed settlement was the equivalent of falling short—a disappointment and an anticlimactic end to litigation. But actually, it is the opposite. There is often just as much satisfaction, if not more, for the client and the lawyers in reaching a good settlement with the other party.

John used to rub his hands together excitedly when we were in the thick of a settlement negotiation, knowing we were close to the end. To settle cases well, it is vitally important to develop a relationship with the lawyer on the other side of the table because the two of you are instrumental in getting the case resolved. If the lawyers cannot find a way to get along, despite the competitive pressures of the situation, then they ordinarily just compound their clients' problems.

David Cupps was no less influential in my development. He was a highly articulate, talented trial lawyer who set a standard for hard work. We worked on a lot of cases together over many years, both when he was at the firm and later when he served as general counsel for a corporate client. Trying to reach the high standards he set was a challenge, and he was sparing in his verbal praise. He instead reflected his confidence in his partners and associates in the work he asked them to undertake in the cases he was handling. His own work was impeccable. Courtrooms would slowly fill as word spread through the courthouse that David Cupps would be conducting an examination or presenting an argument that day. I understood why. One of the first cross-examinations I saw him conduct was so effective and artful I found myself trying in the well of the courtroom to inconspicuously wipe away sleep-deprived tears of admiration I hoped no one else saw.

His writing was inspired and faultless, as he held himself to the same high standards he set for others. People correctly observe that I do an unusual amount of editing when we are preparing briefs and pleadings. Much of that I attribute to David Cupps, who enhanced what I had learned about writing in college and law school, and whose clarity and persuasiveness I can only hope to emulate. When he would ask me about the status of a draft brief on which I was working, and I would tell him, "It's coming out of the typewriter," he would indulge that explanation for delay as a euphemism for the extra attention I was giving the brief, due in no small part to the example he himself had set.

John Elam and David Cupps were not the only people at the firm from whom I learned a great deal. On the contrary, after working with many of the same people for forty-four years, in a firm not known for high turnover, it is safe to say I have learned enormously from virtually everyone at all levels of the Vorys firm with whom I have spent a substantial amount of time. The lawyers, paralegals, secretaries, and administrative personnel at the firm have a wide variety of backgrounds and styles but share a focus on protecting the interests of the firm's clients in an ethical and effective way. It has been a blessing many times over to share the experience of many cases with them.

Staying Fresh

Of course, working at that level is hard to sustain long term, so there is a need for opportunities to step away and recharge. I have been fortunate to have different avocations in life I can switch between—my family, swimming, politics—and that has helped immensely. In fact, I have never really felt burned out. There are times when all the waking hours and energy poured into something can be overwhelming. But actual burnout comes when we lose inspiration for why we are doing something or when we just cannot mentally break through a barrier. In those situations I look for help and motivation across my different interests and just keep working. In my legal cases, I have tried to remind myself why I took on the case. I want to win. Part of it is a competitive urge, but it is for the protection of the client, not just for the sake of competition. I believe in them and want them to achieve the appropriate outcome. Sometimes the reverse is more compelling—when I know there is no way I want to lose this case, and that makes me press forward even harder.

The Value of a Game Plan

Visualization is important in many aspects of our lives. It is a key practice in sports but can be applied to everything, including litigation. It helps if we can visualize ahead of time what it is we want to do and how we want something to go. More often than not, it will work out that way if we develop a game plan beforehand. The technique is a subject of the books of athletes like Michael Phelps, the Olympic-gold-medal swimmer. You simply sit down somewhere, close your eyes, and visualize yourself moving through the events ahead. For a lawyer involved in litigation, that means asking, "What is the purpose? How is the argument going to go? What is the one thing I want to leave with the judges? What is the most important thing about this case? How am I going to express that?" And, of course, it is essential to visualize a good outcome.

Inevitably, there are times when this does not work. No battle plan survives engagement with the adversary, as is said. Surprises happen, and it is necessary to avoid getting flustered. A judge may ask a completely unexpected question; an opposing counsel may make a completely unexpected argument; a witness may give a completely unexpected answer. But if I have been able to visualize what I want to do and remain stoic about any unanticipated developments, I can better maintain the aplomb I need to formulate an effective response.

Recently, we had an intense oral argument in the Supreme Court of Ohio. My colleagues had given me the benefit of extensive preparation, and during the argument, I could tell the justices were fully engaged. They were asking tough and insightful questions, and I had the answers ready, guiding them back to the key points we hoped they would understand about the case. Visualization played a big role in my preparation, allowing me to anticipate the questions and respond confidently and conversationally. It is a powerful tool for a simple reason: Like working backward through a maze, to know the end is to know the route. The case ended in our client's favor.

For an appellate lawyer, game plans must include honesty with judges. Failure to be genuine or truthful can destroy a judge's respect for a lawyer. As an admired friend who served as a trial judge for eighteen years once remarked, the courtroom is a place where you must learn to become comfortable with the truth. She was right. As a lawyer, you must become comfortable with the truth because it is likely to become apparent and decisive in the courtroom, even when it is not as clear or objective as we would like it to be.

My view of judges developed over time, especially as my contemporaries started becoming judges themselves. Many are people whom I have known for years from law practice or other activities in and out of the courtroom. Although they are judges and not direct peers in that context, we share the same lived experience of the law. They will not cut me a break by virtue of our acquaintance with each other. But this mutual understanding allows for open communication in which they feel uninhibited about expressing their thoughts and questions, which I hope I can address just as directly.

Balancing Work and Family

Working all hours and eating take-out dinners most nights was fine for a single guy, but things needed to change when marriage and family came along. Initially, there was just more to do in the same amount of time, so I did not sleep as much—getting up earlier in the morning and staying up later at night. Luckily, I had begun to gain a little seniority, and that meant there were people on my team who could help me. That made a big difference. When the children arrived, parenting became the priority, and I wanted to do that right too. Nobody else can make up for you in that role. But the work still has to get done.

The early years of parenting reminded me of being in school; when you have extracurricular activities, you just become more efficient. Those who were involved in high school or college programs still got everything done. Those activities were important to us and drove us to perform better because we learned how to manage our time and prioritize.

I was fortunate to be at a family-friendly firm. Maryline and I often brought our children into each of our offices for short periods when they were quite young. While our son and daughter might have preferred to be doing something else, it was beneficial for them to see their mother and father at work now and then. The exposure made our jobs less obscure to them and allowed them to get to know many of our colleagues. If you love what you do, you love to *share* it—and that we certainly did.

Our son Adam has told me that one of the things he gained from coming into the office was observing in person the importance of hard work. He could see how, in that environment, effort and diligence were valued and expected. He also loved interacting with my colleagues and learned how to shake hands properly, look people in the eye, form clear sentences, and essentially behave and be treated like an adult. Abigail had the same sorts of experiences in the office and speaks and acts with remarkable maturity as a result. Nonetheless, there necessarily have been many late nights at the firm or on the road, away from my family, over the years.

Getting to Know the People Around Us

Early in my career, staying late at the office led to an ostensible brush with the supernatural. The beloved Mr. Seymour, beset with a terminal illness, died in his office in June 1982. I was in a first-floor conference room that morning, taking a deposition, when the emergency squad arrived outside the windows. It was a sad day for the firm and Mr. Seymour's family. As usual, I stayed at the firm until around ten forty-five that evening, just before the last bus home. Mr. Seymour's office was a few yards away from the elevator on the third floor, on which my office also was located. As I waited for the elevator in the darkened and quiet hallway of the deserted floor, I could plainly hear the distinct sound of paper rustling in his office. Rather than continue to wait for what I imagined might come next, I ran down the adjacent stairway and out the front door, reminding myself that I did not believe in ghosts, but I was unable to unhear what I had just heard. The next morning I was in a nearby restroom at the firm. Suddenly, a small grate in the ceiling just to the left of me swung open overhead. I attributed it to coincidence instead of superstition. But sometimes, I wonder . . .

One of the few regrets from my time at the law firm is that I did not take the initiative to get to know Mr. Seymour when the opportunity had presented itself in my early months as an associate—a sentiment I felt acutely the day he died. I mistakenly rationalized my hesitation by attributing it to his preeminence and my newcomer status, as well as his ill health. I wish I had gotten to know him. I sensed in him a kindred spirit, not only because of his professional accomplishments but especially due to his restless soul, adventurous travels, and occasional indifference to conventional expectations. Several of my colleagues who knew him well have told me from time to time over the years that I remind them of Mr. Seymour in various ways, which I have taken as a compliment but which makes me regret all the more the opportunity I let go by.

Along that same line, I remember by contrast how glad I was to have taken a few moments one Friday evening many years later to ask our associate Jocelyn Prewitt-Stanley about the beautiful roses that had been delivered to her that day, when I saw them on her desk as she and I were both heading out of the office. They were from her husband for her birthday, she said—a short conversation I especially treasured when Jocelyn (who was pregnant at the time) went into premature labor and tragically died during childbirth that weekend.

The moral of both stories is to take the time to get to know the people with whom we are working when the circumstances arise because we all mean more to each other than we may realize. We postpone that opportunity at our own peril.

Chapter 7:
Supreme Court Case

The Road to the Supreme Court

Since it was founded in 1909, the Vorys law firm has presented three cases in the Supreme Court of the United States. The first one was in the 1920s when the firm represented the brother of the attorney general for President Warren G. Harding, who got into a disagreement with the Senate on a subpoena issue. The firm next had a case there in the 1980s. It was a workers' compensation matter that involved the balance between federal and state authority at atomic energy production facilities. The third case was heard and decided in 2022.

That third case—the most recent case—arose because a commercial renal dialysis provider maintained that the Medicare Secondary Payer Act allowed it to force employer group health plans to pay more than they otherwise would spend for kidney dialysis treatments. At least one employer health benefit plan believed that interpretation was wrong and could be ruinous.

Dialysis is an expensive course of medical treatment. An individual who has end-stage renal disease needs dialysis three times a week for the rest of his or her life. The sheer volume of the treatment means it can be an expensive process—way too expensive for almost any individual to bear alone. Many group health plans provide kidney dialysis coverage. In such instances, the cost of dialysis becomes one of the expenses group health plans must bear in serving the 157 million Americans who depend upon them to cover the bulk of their health-care costs.

Group health plans normally seek to control their costs (to minimize premiums and spread coverage over a wider range of medical conditions) by creating networks of medical care providers for their members. Most medical care providers are interested in being part of a network because of the volume of patients their inclusion in the network will bring them; in exchange, they offer to provide services at a negotiated lower cost. For reasons peculiar to their sector, however, dialysis providers often will not enter into network agreements with group health plans. Employer group health plans that provide dialysis coverage in those circumstances must be vigilant in guarding against exploitation.

Congress had enacted the Medicare Secondary Payer Act in recognition of the fact that many dialysis patients are covered by both Medicare and an employer group health plan. Under the Medicare law, which generally provides benefits only once an individual reaches age sixty-five, a person who has end-stage renal disease can qualify for Medicare at any age. The Medicare Secondary Payer Act provides that if such an individual is covered both by an employer group health plan and Medicare, the group health plan pays first, and Medicare pays the balance of the reasonable cost of dialysis.

The interpretation of the law espoused by the dialysis providers could have resulted in group health plans having to pay enormous costs for renal dialysis patients, which would consume resources needed for them and everybody else who depends on the finite resources of a group health plan. Every dollar paid for excessive charges for dialysis is a dollar that cannot help with another medical need.

When the administrator of the group health plan came to our firm for help, my colleagues took the case and successfully litigated it in the district court, where they won. The dialysis provider then took the case to the United States Court of Appeals for the Sixth Circuit. My colleagues asked if I would help prepare them for the oral argument in the court of appeals in my capacity as a leader of the firm's appellate subgroup.

My colleagues did an excellent job preparing and presenting the oral argument in the court of appeals. But even so, the three-judge court went the other way. It was a split decision, two to one. Two of the three judges adopted the interpretation of the Medicare Secondary Payer Act the dialysis provider had urged. One judge dissented. His dissent expressed the logic of the literal interpretation of the Medicare Secondary Payer Act quite clearly. The majority opinion was a disappointment. As with most such disappointments in the context of litigation, it only meant the lawyers must identify and evaluate potential next steps.

The dissent gave us the confidence to continue. Everything was at stake. Our client was a third-party administrator for an employer group health plan. The third-party administrator processes the claims according to the coverage rules adopted by the group health plan—a decision that can have a monumental impact on an individual's life and family and other members of the group health plan. There was only one potential way out of the ruling handed down by the Court of Appeals.

Petitioning the Supreme Court to Hear the Case

Every case is important to the parties involved, but few cases are important to everybody else. What the Supreme Court looks for are cases that are critical to the entire nation. I had thought from the outset the case had the potential to go to the Supreme Court. I told my colleague Rodney Holaday as much when I helped him prepare for the oral argument in the court of appeals. Rodney was the lawyer who had been leading the charge on the case as it came up through the district court and the court of appeals. I got the briefs and saw the importance of the issue—whether a group health plan that provides uniform reimbursement of dialysis expenses, regardless of whether the patients have end-stage renal disease, observes the standards of the Medicare Secondary Payer Act. Once I understood what the issue was, I saw it had never been finally resolved. It instead had been percolating around different lower courts, without a uniform final answer, which gave it the ingredients of a case in which the Supreme Court might be interested. There was a huge amount at stake, as Medicare is one of the largest programs of the federal government, and group health plans cover 157 million Americans.

When my colleagues and I got the decision from the court of appeals and saw the excellent dissent, we knew it could resonate with the Supreme Court. Then, around the same time, there was a similar case in the United States Court of Appeals for the Ninth Circuit, which covers several Western states, in which the court went the other way from the Sixth Circuit majority, taking essentially the same position as our client and the dissenting judge in the Sixth Circuit. Thus, there was a so-called circuit split, which meant that something that was lawful in California was unlawful in Ohio under the same statute. That is a classic situation that the Supreme Court steps in to clarify.

It is a challenge to get a case into the Supreme Court. The party seeking review must file a petition for a writ of certiorari, which the other side can oppose. In 2021, the year we filed, there were approximately eight thousand certiorari petitions—eight thousand cases litigants had asked the court to take—and the court took only eighty. The odds were about one in a hundred. But we felt positive about the chances because of the circuit split and the potential impact of the decision on so many people.

We filed our certiorari briefs and waited as the Supreme Court decided whether to take the case. The clerk of the court publishes information about the date on which the justices are going to consider and vote on the certiorari petition. The petitioner needs four votes; at least four of the nine justices must vote to take the case. The court has complete discretion as to which such cases to take. On the date the court originally was supposed to decide whether to take our case, the justices relisted it, or "held it over for the next conference," which we thought might be a good sign because it meant they may be taking an even closer look at it, making sure it was an appropriate case to accept.

Decisions on certiorari petitions are usually issued on Monday mornings at ten, so we were ready for that. But the preceding Friday afternoon, at about four thirty, I got an email on my desktop computer from the clerk of the Supreme Court. The subject line was "A new docket entry has been added." With my heart racing, I clicked on the link, opened it up, and scrolled down the docket. And there, at the bottom, it said "Petition GRANTED." It was an electrifying and unforgettable moment. It meant the Supreme Court was going to take the case and give our beleaguered client an opportunity to challenge the ruling of the Sixth Circuit. It was an exciting breakthrough for our client and everyone on the team, including Rodney, who had gotten away for a short bike ride, only to have his cell phone "start buzzing like crazy," causing him to pull over to check his messages. We got to work right away on the next steps.

Working with the Solicitor General

The Supreme Court put the case on a fast track, and we had to turn around the merits brief quickly. Shortly after we filed the brief, the solicitor general of the United States came into the case on our side, on behalf of the Biden administration, which was another truly exciting moment. The solicitor general has the opportunity to intervene in cases, especially ones that involve the interpretation of federal statutes. A couple of weeks beforehand, we went through a rigorous presentation process with the solicitor general's team to convince them they ought to have an interest in the case. The other side, of course, went through a similar process, presenting the opposite position. A couple of days before Christmas, we got a late-afternoon email that announced that the solicitor general was coming into the case on our client's side.

Building Our Team

We built our team quickly. In addition to the three lawyers who already were working on the case, the guiding principle was to find subject-matter experts (on Medicare, employer group health plans, and appellate procedure). I did not want or need to be the strongest person on the team. I have long made it my objective to look for lawyers who I think are smarter, more perceptive, or more hardworking than me. In the end there were nine people at the firm who were substantially involved in the briefing and preparation for the oral argument. They were all lawyers who were utterly proficient in their respective areas of expertise. None of them were prone to letting me off the hook. It was an intense process. We did nearly a dozen mock arguments, with lawyers reading the briefs and then asking the hardest questions they could imagine. And they *had* to be tough too. Our opposing counsel would be addressing the Supreme Court for the eighty-first time.

Arguing the Case

In addressing the Supreme Court, as with so many other activities, preparation is the pathway to excellence. Our opposition was highly experienced. I was a neophyte at that level. But we had the advantage of a client who had done the right thing, an excellent set of briefs, the backing of the solicitor general, and the hunger of a highly talented appellate team. What was also obvious was that our opposition saw our client as a force to be reckoned with and produced a formidable stack of amicus curiae ("friend of the court") briefs, which are briefs nonparties can file to assist a court, from leading lawyers and organizations across the nation, urging the court to reject our position.

We had been preparing for the oral argument for weeks in Columbus. On the Thursday before the oral argument, set for Tuesday, March 1, 2022, we went to Washington. My colleagues virtually locked me in a hotel room and asked me tough questions all weekend. As would be expected, the questions covered the complex workings of the group health plan, the Medicare law generally, the way the lower courts had handled the issues, and the arguments presented in the other side's briefs and the numerous amicus briefs. The prolonged drills showed abundant foresight. The justices themselves asked many of the same questions at the oral argument.

With the benefit of the team's assistance, I could not have been better prepared. I allowed myself no distractions, even to the extent that Maryline and Adam and Abigail were staying in a different hotel because they knew we were going to be focused on the preparations. But it was comforting to know they were nearby.

Our hotel was near the Supreme Court. Mindful of the experience of a legendary Supreme Court advocate who had made it to the courthouse only by sheer luck after an unexpected heavy snowstorm several years ago, I wanted to be able to walk in case it was snowing that day. We each had our own room, but we also had one large room—our "war room"—set up like a boardroom. Every morning, after everyone took care of their other business, we would come in and take up where we had left off in our ongoing conversation about the case. Each session evolved into a torrent of difficult questions. Others from the firm took part by Teams or Zoom calls and would help brainstorm possible questions of law and fact. The team was quite intellectually diverse, with specialists in each of the subjects the case involved; everyone had a unique outlook on the issues with which we were dealing. It was perfect preparation.

The Saturday afternoon before the oral argument, Rodney and I took a walk and ended up sitting on the steps of the Supreme Court building, looking out over Washington. It was a beautiful, sunny day. I asked Rodney, "Did you ever dream this case would be here?"

"Honestly . . . no," he said, "because it started out just like any other case."

But he and the rest of the team had been diligent. My colleagues responsible for the case in the district court and court of appeals had done their jobs impeccably. They had done things the *right* way; they had never cut corners. The importance of attention to detail and having done things the right way, which I had learned as a young associate, becomes paramount when a case goes to the Supreme Court. Everything is scrutinized. Any mistake, oversight, or misstep could have been exploited by the opposing side. Our team's meticulous work stood strong, passing with flying colors, a true vindication of the effort they had exerted all along.

That moment sitting outside was one of the few breaks I got that weekend. At one point I arranged with Maryline that I would take a break for an hour and go out for a walk with her, Adam, and Abigail. They came to the room at the appointed time . . . when my colleagues and I were right in the middle of a very intense Q&A grilling. They sat there for a little bit and took in how intense it was. They soon left us to it, saying, "Okay, we'll see you later." It was good for them to be there, even for a few minutes, just to see what that was like.

On the morning of the argument, we all went together to the plaza of the Supreme Court. It was a buoyant moment. At one point in our team's bantering, Adam turned to me and aptly said, "I bet you're 100 percent focused on the argument." It was soon time to enter the courthouse. At that point—March 2022—the nation was still emerging from the COVID-19 pandemic, and the courthouse was closed to the public. We were allowed two lawyers per side, period. No clients, no other lawyers, no friends, no family, no public. Inside the courtroom, it was just the justices, their law clerks, two lawyers per side, and a limited number of journalists. Face masks were required except when speaking.

My family (Abigail, Maryline, and Adam) and I stand on the steps of the US Supreme Court building before the oral argument I presented that morning.

The exterior of the court building is clad in white marble, as are most of its main hallways. Having passed through security, we were ushered into an ornate waiting room until the marshal came to escort us to the courtroom. The waiting room is a stately chamber facing an elegant interior courtyard at the Supreme Court. The walls are full of portraits of previous justices and famous advocates. With a bronze statue of Daniel Webster watching directly over me, my co-counsel and I sat there with our opposing counsel, reading through our notes and soaking up the history all around us.

Our case was the second argument on the docket that morning. We were able to listen to the livestreamed first argument and knew when it was done. Then, it was our turn. The marshal came to get us and walked us to the courtroom. The doors opened. The justices awaited us. I walked in and went straight to the podium. We were the petitioners, so I would be speaking first. All the preparation had been for that moment. Standing there while waiting until the justices were ready, I reflected on the courage of our client, the teamwork at the firm, and everyone who had helped get us ready. Chief Justice John G. Roberts Jr. called my name, indicating I should proceed.

During an oral argument at the Supreme Court, the justices in recent years have given the advocate two minutes at the beginning to make an uninterrupted statement. They then start asking questions. The order of the questions ordinarily is determined by seniority. The questions come in rapid fire. Sometimes, I was in the middle of an answer to the question of one justice when a different justice asked another question. I would shift to that question, but the objective was to respond, explain, and then pivot back to the main point that needed to be made.

All the preparation and practice were profoundly helpful. The justices asked questions that were quite demanding. How did the group health plan work? What coverages are available in certain scenarios? What do certain provisions of the Medicare Secondary Payer Act mean? What is your response to the other side's interpretation? What about certain hypothetical situations? I answered to the best of my ability. Almost all the justices asked me penetrating questions. My law school classmate, Justice

Sonia Sotomayor, was particularly rigorous, as was Justice Elena Kagan. The argument went over the originally allotted time, which we shared with the assistant to the solicitor general. I loved every minute of it and wished it could have gone longer.

In many ways, the experience was like the mental training that endurance sports require. When you are in the oral argument, for the first minute or two, you have to get through the metaphorical wall. But then, once the process starts—if you are prepared—the argument takes on its own flow and momentum. About ten minutes into the argument, the thought went through my mind that this was just like any other oral argument except we were in the Supreme Court of the United States. The cadence, the pattern, and the flow are the same as in any other appellate proceeding. The difference is, in the Supreme Court, you look at the nine justices and realize they have the last word.

After the argument concluded, we gathered the ceremonial quill pens the marshal customarily puts on the counsel table for the lawyers who appear. I told my opposing counsel how deeply I envied the number of arguments he had presented to the Supreme Court, and then went back to the hotel, where the team was still assembled in the conference room. Everyone who had worked on the case with me in Washington was there, along with Maryline and Abigail. They all had been following the livestream of the oral argument online. When a question was posed, my colleagues often anticipated the answer, thanks to our thorough preparation. Unbeknownst to me, colleagues in the firm's offices around the nation had organized livestream broadcasts and also had followed the argument. Adam had been listening intently to the livestream from his law firm's office in Washington. During his law school years, he had read many Supreme Court opinions and briefs, so he was acquainted with what was unfolding. He later said he could tell how much I was enjoying the argument from listening to it.

The room was charged with excitement. The team brought out a bottle of champagne. We shared our reflections on the experience, feeling a profound sense of gratitude for the opportunity the Supreme Court and our client had given us and, on my part, for the excellent teamwork that had made such a difference. Checkout time loomed, however, cutting us short, but we savored that moment together.

Then came the most harrowing phase of any such experience—the days after the oral argument, when the lawyer thinks of additional points they could have made, of better ways to have said things, of implications of questions the court had asked. Little can be done about any of those concerns after the fact because the case is in the hands of the court at that point. Fortunately, in this case the argument took place near the close of the term (which regularly ends in June), so we had reason to believe the wait for the decision would not be overly long.

Decisive Victory

We learned the result just after ten in the morning on June 21, 2022. The Supreme Court issues its opinions on designated days. The first opinion ordinarily is posted at ten, followed by any others at ten-minute intervals. A throng of observers (thousands of Supreme Court aficionados around the world) customarily gathers online at scotusblog.com, especially in the last days of June as the court's annual term nears its end, to follow the release of the opinions.

The opinion in our case was the first one issued that morning. It was a very good decision for our client—unanimous on all but one point, which the court also decided in our favor by a vote of seven to two. We immediately confirmed with the client representatives, who also had been following online. Congratulatory emails started pouring in. Shortly after the Supreme Court issued its decision, the New York Stock Exchange temporarily suspended trading in our opponent's shares, which had plummeted in value. That gave great practical emphasis to the importance of the decision.

For everyone on our team, there was immense satisfaction in knowing our client's clear victory translated into a win for all 157 million people who depend upon group health plans. One thing that struck me in the process was how often the Supreme Court addresses Medicare and Medicaid cases.

Those cases rarely make headlines due to their technical complexity and lack of sensationalism compared to issues like affirmative action, abortion, immigration, or presidential immunity. (For example, the controversial opinion in *Dobbs v. Jackson Women's Health Organization*, which overruled the reproductive rights recognized in *Roe v. Wade*, came out just two days later and is still a subject of national debate.) However, Medicare and Medicaid decisions have at least as much practical importance to the majority of Americans.

Through it all, I remained grateful to the anonymous taxi driver in Washington whose advice to "count your blessings," coming one day before the oral argument, could not have been more timely or perfect.

Maryline and I pose for a photo together before attending the annual dinner of the Supreme Court Historical Society, June 2023.

Chapter 8:
Political Commitment

Hand in hand with my aspiration to become a lawyer, political engagement has been a significant part of my life since I was in grade school. It started in a small way, a few years after watching the 1960 election returns as a first grader. In the fall of 1965, when I was eleven years old, a civically active neighbor paid her son and me fifty cents an hour to deliver the Democratic Party tabloid for the upcoming municipal election to all the homes in our subdivision. After a weekend of work, her son and I had each made several dollars—it turned out to be the only time I have ever made any money in politics—but that was not the only thing I liked about the process. I remember the fascination of going door to door in our neighborhood and on the adjacent streets. It gave me a real, if fleeting, glimpse into the importance of the lives, interests, and needs of the people around me. Over the following years, I volunteered in many other campaigns and became more and more exposed to the operations of local—and national—politics.

In October 1970, when I was sixteen, President Richard M. Nixon came to Columbus for a campaign rally at the Ohio Statehouse for the midterm elections. It was an extraordinary event for the president to come to town in that era, and even though it was a school day, several classmates and I managed to get the necessary permission to go and see him. Four of us made our way to the rally. I wrote about the experience in my application for the Ohio Governor's School a few months later: "During the speech, the turmoil which now grips the nation was very evident. On one side, antiwar protestors were shouting slogans; on the other side, 'Silent Majority' members were glaring their contempt for them. 40,000 people had come to hear the speech but, amidst the hostility, hardly anyone listened to it. Afterward, however, small groups of people gathered on the State House lawn and talked about America's problems. By listening to each other we all learned a lot."

After the speech, President Nixon started to work the crowd line. Being young and heedless of courtesy, the four of us managed to make our way to the front. The president stopped to shake my hand. We spoke briefly, and I admired his cufflinks. He seemed pleased about that and reached into his coat pocket and pulled out his pen, then gave it to me as a souvenir. I could not believe it; the president had given me his actual pen. It was elegant. I kept it safe and later got it mounted below a framed photo of President Nixon and his family. I still have it.

I had supported Richard Nixon's election to the presidency in 1968, as a high school freshman. It seemed to me he and a new administration would have a better ability to end the Vietnam War than the incumbent Democratic administration, in which his worthy opponent (Hubert H. Humphrey) was serving as vice president.

The Making of a Democrat

My thoughts began to change in 1971 as a participant in the Ohio Governors School. That experience proved to be a political awakening. At the age of seventeen, I got direct insight into state government policies and close exposure to leading figures of the state government and the Ohio Democratic Party. It was a time of progressive ferment at the state government level. Governor John J. Gilligan was an exceptionally bright and dedicated political leader, whose determination led to the enactment of a series of progressive reforms that modernized the state government and, in my opinion, put the State of Ohio in a much better position to serve its people's needs.

At the time, the funding of our state universities and primary and secondary schools was strained. Environmental protection was inadequate, and the infrastructure (including roads and bridges) was deteriorating. Republicans who had dominated Ohio politics for years were focused on cutting taxes and limiting government activity. That policy resonated with the conservative instincts of many Ohioans but put the state government at an impasse in terms of promoting the public good in the face of new day-to-day challenges the people of Ohio faced.

When Governor Gilligan took office, he brought about sweeping changes at a fast pace. They included an Environmental Protection Agency, ethics reform, and a new state income tax, along with substantial property tax reform. Primary and secondary schools were better funded, as were the state universities. Civil rights legislation was strengthened at the state level. Equality of opportunity became more achievable. The rights of union members were better protected. Many such fundamental changes were made under his leadership, promptly and as a concerted effort.

Governor Gilligan strongly influenced my rookie view of politics and politicians. Because it was all I knew firsthand, his leadership led me to take for granted that everybody in politics was like him. He was erudite and well-spoken, exuding a healthy love of the political process. His Catholicism and interest in policy and moral philosophy also appealed to me. At the time, Ohio was falling behind the rest of the nation in terms of keeping up with modern life. Governor Gilligan seemed like a breath of fresh air in a coherent, organized, and wholesome way. He and his administration made a big and positive impact on me and on the state of Ohio. It was an uplifting environment in which to become more immersed in politics and is one reason why I have been a Democrat ever since.

Campaign Volunteer

As I got older, I became more involved with the Democratic Party and took on greater levels of responsibility. I volunteered and worked actively in 1971 for the election of one of the first women ever to serve on the Columbus City Council, Fran Ryan, at a time when women were still an exception as political candidates and officeholders. I served as a precinct captain for the Democratic Party in the OSU area, volunteered as a campus organizer for the George McGovern for President campaign in 1972, and worked on the campaign of the local Democratic candidate for the Ohio House of Representatives. I was honored when Dr. Sweet enlisted me in his campaign when he sought the Democratic nomination for a seat in Congress in 1976.

In law school, I took the train from New Haven and spent a weekend in Rhode Island helping my friend and classmate Peter Kougasian in his father's campaign for reelection to the Cranston School Committee. Peter's classic flair for quick-witted humor showed itself the moment we emerged from the train station, when I asked who the Civil War–era statue outside the entrance portrayed as a man on horseback. "That's my father's opponent," he said.

In the course of these volunteer activities, I helped to circulate candidacy petitions for Democrats seeking to get on the ballot, assisted with raising money, and took part in phone banks and envelope-stuffing for mass mailings—all of which gave me a good education in the rudiments of the political process. It also felt like a much-needed contribution to civic progress when I helped in 1987 with the campaign of Janet E. Jackson, the first Black woman to be elected as a judge of the Franklin County Municipal Court.

Even nominally prosaic tasks could be far more interesting than expected. In 1982, as a young lawyer, I volunteered as the driver for the Democratic gubernatorial candidate for the closing months of the campaign when he was in central and southern Ohio. His name was Richard F. Celeste. He was an extraordinarily bright, charismatic, and engaging figure who had already held a series of important diplomatic and legislative positions. While on the road with him and others traveling with him, I learned a lot about public policy and practical politics. I was indebted to him for that opportunity. I could see what excellence looked like, which he continued to demonstrate during two terms as governor.

As I immersed myself in college and law school, academics became my priority. But my early political experiences informed my study of both history and law by grounding each in the reality of day-to-day life from a grassroots perspective. Making an effort to understand the actual circumstances of judges, juries, and the people with whom you live side by side is indispensable. Politics, when done right, offers a similar experience. From an early age, it has exposed me to a broad range of people, places, ideas, issues, needs, and circumstances I would not otherwise have encountered. When I realized that history and law move through each of us as individuals in the places where we live and work, it animated my interest in the political process and helped with my studies in school. As with history, learning about the judicial system and the political process becomes far more realistic and meaningful when done in real-world settings.

I like to think these early experiences gave me a more realistic view of politics. Through occasional hard knocks, they also inoculated me against the disillusionment that can set in upon discovering that, generally speaking, people in politics are no better or worse than people in any other occupation, and people who feel one way about an issue or candidate are not necessarily superior to people who feel another way. We all have faults and shortcomings, and I am certainly no exception. Through watching others, I became cautious about casting judgment on fellow citizens and saw the need to avoid becoming so consumed by politics that it turns into its own reality.

The Gary Hart Campaign

I grew by leaps and bounds when given the opportunity to coordinate the Ohio campaign of Senator Gary W. Hart for the Democratic presidential nomination in 1984. I knew of the Colorado senator by reputation, not only in the national news media but also at Yale Law School, from which he had graduated in 1964. Then, I met him through his classmate and national campaign manager, Oliver "Pudge" Henkel, the lawyer from Cleveland whom I knew from his recruiting activity on behalf of the Jones Day law firm. Pudge and his wife Sally invited me to their home when Senator Hart was there. I got to know him in person in that setting. The more I talked with Senator Hart, the more I thought he would make a superb president. When the campaign came about and Pudge asked if I would be the Ohio campaign manager, I jumped at the chance.

I posed for a photo with Lee Hart and Senator Gary Hart outside Cleveland Hopkins Airport, September 1983.

Distinguished by the new ideas and approaches he brought into policy debates, Senator Hart was an incisive and fresh thinker on everything from national security to diplomatic policy, US intelligence capabilities, postindustrial economic growth, and social welfare programs. His method of politics emphasized grassroots personal contact and direct conversations with voters. That resonated deeply with me—and still does to this day. As Theodore H. White wrote in *The Making of the President 1972* about Gary Hart's leadership as national manager of the McGovern campaign, "Hart loved his organization as a painter does a canvas—touching, retouching, refining, admiring his own art." His focus on military reform sparked a corresponding interest on my part to learn more through brief service in the Ohio Military Reserve, which functions as an organized reserve force for the Ohio National Guard through training to assist the state and local governments during emergencies.

One of the front-runners for the 1984 Democratic nomination was Senator John H. Glenn Jr. from Ohio. That made involvement in an Ohio campaign for one of his rivals somewhat awkward. Senator Glenn was beloved in Ohio not only as a national hero for his achievement as the first American to have orbited the Earth but also for his service in the United States Senate since 1975. My intuition told me his presidential campaign nonetheless would not make it to the Ohio primary, leaving the field open. That would give other candidates, including Senator Hart, a chance to win the Ohio delegates to the Democratic National Convention if they were prepared for that circumstance to arise. The other major candidates with significant staying power and support were former Vice President Walter F. Mondale and Reverend Jesse Jackson, who had come to prominence as a civil rights leader.

Assembling the team while Senator Glenn was in the race was challenging. Understandably, most active Ohio Democrats were supporting the Glenn campaign and averse to aiding a competitor. I traveled across the state, meeting supporters in their homes and enlisting them in the campaign one by one. Our ranks included a handyman, a plumber, students, teachers, environmentalists, lawyers, and others. Almost all were, like me, sincerely interested in the Hart campaign but not possessed of a great deal of political experience. Many had never had any prior political involvement, or had been left out of the political process, but proved to be no less able to function successfully in it. We met at kitchen tables, fast-food restaurants, public libraries, and other such places.

Initially, our team was small enough that the organizing effort required only one desk file. But personal effort eventually succeeded. Persistence in active recruitment and following up on leads allowed us to form the nucleus of a large enough campaign to get Senator Hart on the Ohio ballot. That required lining up a slate of delegate candidates and obtaining sufficient petition signatures in each of Ohio's twenty-one congressional districts to meet the statutory requirements. In addition, we had to challenge the Ohio Democratic Party delegate selection plan, which the Democratic National Committee ordered the state party to partially rewrite. We also took steps to minimize the advantage other candidates would gain from the selection of "superdelegates" who would be more inclined to support an establishment-backed candidate rather than an upstart such as Senator Hart, who was challenging the establishment.

My fellow Hart supporters and I were a well-motivated collection of, for the most part, novices and amateurs. As *The Washington Post* archly noted in a story about one of our early meetings with Senator Hart at the Cleveland airport, "The eight volunteers were young: Mr. Hart's campaign coordinator in Ohio is just a few years out of law school." A respected columnist for *The Columbus Citizen-Journal* accurately described me as "an active if obscure Democratic player before this year." *The New York Times* skeptically reported that neither I nor my Indiana counterpart "had prior national political experience." We were plainly in over our heads, so we necessarily made it up as we went along. For lack of an alternative, we operated on the principle that fortune favors the bold. In such situations you have no choice but to figure out what is required and do it.

Then Senator Hart won the New Hampshire primary, a week after placing unexpectedly well in the Iowa caucuses. Our bare-bones organization had to ramp up quickly. A reporter for *The Plain Dealer*, the major Cleveland newspaper, noted I told him that, before the Iowa caucuses, "this was Hart headquarters, pulling a not-very-fat file folder from a desk in his law offices." That changed dramatically. As the *Akron Beacon Journal* reported, "For eight months, John Kulewicz ran Hart's Ohio campaign out of a cardboard box ferried between his Columbus law office and his apartment." But "since last week and Hart's upset victory in the New Hampshire primary, more than 1,000 calls have poured into Kulewicz's office and the homes of campaign workers across the state," and "his office floor has turned into one big filing cabinet."

I told the reporter, "We're still living off the land, but the land has gotten much more bountiful. It has been overwhelming, and also very gratifying, for the volunteers who have been with us since the early days when we had to close off rooms [in the campaign headquarters] to conserve heat." It was an exciting, fast-paced period. Night after night, when I got home to the Olentangy Village apartment in which I was living, I opened a mailbox full of offers of help, supportive letters, and unsolicited campaign contributions.

We maintained the strategy we had pursued from the outset. "We have always built our effort on the assumption he would be the most viable candidate at the time of the Ohio primary and we will continue to go on that assumption," I told the *Akron Beacon Journal*. We sought to attract particular attention to Senator Hart's industrial strategy. It spoke directly to the concerns of many Ohio Democrats that the continuation of previous policies would not adequately address the transformation of the Ohio economy and its disruptive effect on the jobs and lives of hundreds of thousands of Ohio families. Senator Hart was an early proponent of training for new jobs and using technology and information to grow job opportunities in a new economy.

By seeking to empower Americans who were not political professionals, he also tapped into a massive, unspoken yearning for a way to refresh the sense of national greatness and purpose that victory in World War II had given our nation. Gary Hart was the first major presidential candidate who had come of age in the 1960s. But his appeal was not merely generational. As our wide-ranging team in Ohio reflected, the inspiration of his candidacy reached across the spectrum. He offered hope to Americans, animated by the promise of the postwar United States, who were looking for a way through what Bruce Springsteen subsequently called "the fall from Eden in the long, slow afterburn of the 1960s" that characterized "'70s post-Vietnam America." Gary Hart caught on because he provided a constructive way for millions of Americans to reinvigorate the country they loved.

I learned the job of campaign manager on the fly. Among other ways of doing so, I went to New Hampshire a few days before its primary to check out the organizing effort there and learn what the state coordinator (Jeanne Shaheen, who later became governor and senator) was doing. Things were moving so fast that the knowledge gap on my part was not as intimidating as it otherwise could have been.

The most crucial aspect up to that point had been knowing the deadlines, understanding the calendar, and getting the slate of delegates on the ballot. That involved a huge amount of legwork and meeting people. After getting that job done, we eventually received reinforcements from the national campaign. We sought to help them understand the points that were most relevant to Ohio voters, sharing what was important to people locally and traveling around the state with them.

The campaign that followed was a frenetic and satisfactory experience for all involved. We ended up with a team of three thousand volunteers in eleven field offices across the state. We were multigenerational and multiracial. Women and men served in leadership roles. Applying the principle of learning the world through your feet, we made an extensive door-to-door campaign the centerpiece of our efforts. We supplemented that organization and field effort with the limited television advertising the campaign could afford (commercials filmed in Ohio with our guidance) and many rallies and other campaign appearances by Senator Hart and surrogates on his behalf.

We kept our substantive focus on the new ideas Senator Hart offered the Democratic Party. Students on college campuses from Ohio University to Cleveland State University enlivened the campaign. They insisted on substantive answers to pointed questions and responded with enthusiasm when they understood they were being taken seriously. Industrial union members took the campaign as a way to send a message to the Democratic Party establishment that new thinking was essential for the protection of their jobs and preservation of their bargaining units. Across the state, Ohioans who were determined to resist the fading of the American dream came forward to help and to vote for Gary Hart.

Elsewhere in the nation, the tide was running against us. The morning of the May 8 Ohio primary, the grim headline in *The Washington Post* read, "Hart, Trailing in Polls, Pins Hope for Survival on Ohio Upset." The political columnist for *The Columbus Citizen-Journal* observed that "Ohio for Gary Hart is a Rubicon, his last chance to prove he can win in an industrial northern state, the final ledge before the abyss of virtual mathematical elimination." Many pundits thought, as one veteran Hart organizer later wrote, that "any realistic chance of securing the nomination ended" several days earlier with a loss in the Texas primary.

The next morning, however, the jubilant headline in the *Akron Beacon Journal* exclaimed, "A horse race again! Hart wins Ohio." Against all odds, we came from behind to victory, winning the primary election for Senator Hart with 43 percent of the vote, the balance being split between Vice President Mondale and Reverend Jackson. It was a vote for a new direction for the Democratic Party. The result was almost exactly what I had privately predicted over the preceding weekend, based on an intuitive extrapolation from the poll conducted by a veteran *Columbus Dispatch* reporter. When I shared that prediction with the press corps (before learning to clear things like that with the national campaign office), the national press secretary said, "I don't know where he got that."

Senator Hart told his celebrating Ohio volunteers on election night, "You have changed the course of American history. I hope all of you will treasure tonight." As we let the upset victory sink in, I told our gathering in Columbus that "the Democrats of Ohio have taken the lead in bringing this nation into a new era of leadership." Later, Senator Hart recounted, "I was so happy that night. I felt exhilarated and vindicated. The people of this country never gave up on me. I kept thinking about all that John Kulewicz had been going through in Ohio. And I was so happy for our people, our hardcore supporters because it wasn't just vindicating me; it was vindicating them."

Gary Hart did so well in the Ohio primary that Ohio had the second-largest contingent of Hart delegates to the Democratic National Convention that year (behind California). I served as vice chair of the Ohio delegation, helping to keep the Hart delegates lined up for roll-call votes on the party platform and other issues and poised to build on our voting strength as a bloc if lightning were to strike. "It was, in fact, the Ohio primary that brought this campaign to San Francisco," Senator Hart pointed out in a meeting with the entire Ohio delegation at a convention breakfast.

It was a team effort that went perfectly and was one of the best teams I ever put together. I had to find people to help the campaign and then learn to delegate to them. I came to have profound respect for what a highly motivated corps of hardworking people can accomplish when they focus on the objective. As I told the reporter for *The Columbus Dispatch* on the way from the Ohio secretary of state's office to the victory celebration on the night of the primary election, "I'm actually just a very small cog in a very large wheel that did very well for Senator Hart today."

Two other lessons were aptly articulated for me by others. David Cupps told me shortly after I got back to the law firm from the primary election that "the conclusion you should draw from that experience is that politics is a game best played by amateurs." Another gentleman, a prominent Cleveland lawyer and senior statesman of the Ohio Democratic Party, wagged his finger at me a few weeks later and said, with a touch of good-natured humor, "The only reason you people won is you had no idea there was no way you could win." I took their words of wisdom to heart.

In addition, I was grateful for the patience of my colleagues at the law firm. All this happened just a few years into my law career. I had started at the firm in January 1981 and had become quite busy with the cases in which I was involved. The campaign started out small but eventually got to the point where I had to take a leave of absence from work. My original intent had been to do legal work in the first half of the day and then run the campaign in the late afternoon and evening. But the plan did not work out that way; the campaign just started cascading. It was apparent to everybody. TV news crews were coming through for interviews; there were constant phone calls, people coming in for meetings; letters and contributions were pouring in. It was untenable to try to practice law at the same time. I had not planned to become a full-time campaign manager, but events were gradually leaving me no choice.

On one typical day—this was back when there were telephones with multiple lines and secretaries to answer them—my secretary came into a meeting and said, "John, I've got Governor Celeste on line one and CBS News on line two. Which one do you want to take?" (I talked with

Governor Celeste, of course.) That sort of situation was becoming a daily occurrence, so it was obvious I had a big decision to make. Nobody else could easily take over the campaign at that point because I had organized it and knew everybody. To abandon all we had accomplished so far would have been a real disappointment and genuine setback for our efforts. It was also obvious I could not get much work done at the firm.

One other circumstance cast the die. In those days, we could forward our home phones to our office phones, which is what I normally did because a lot of campaign calls were coming to me at my home number. Unfortunately, I forwarded it to my law firm phone one weekend morning when I was delayed getting to the office to be able to pick it up, so incoming calls were bouncing from my office phone and ringing through the whole firm until someone answered. One of my colleagues was trying to get some weekend work done at the office and conscientiously picked up one incoming call after another. He was a brilliant lawyer and good friend but a gruff sort and soon reached the limits of his patience. When another unwitting caller then rang and asked if I was there, he had had enough and barked, "No, he is not here, but every f***ing idiot in the Western Hemisphere is trying to reach him." Something had to change.

I was young and single and had few bills, so I could afford to take an unpaid leave and work full-time in politics (also unpaid) for a couple months. It was a big risk, but the excitement and competitive thrill of the campaign, along with my respect for Senator Hart's ideas, record, and background, motivated me to go for it.

The conversation with my colleagues about taking an unpaid leave was quick. Our managing partner, John Elam, was out of the country, and it was not as easy then to reach someone overseas as it is now. So I spoke with my work coordinator, Sue Richards, and explained what I needed to do. (As fate would have it, Sue is also the colleague with whom I spoke three years later when Maryline and I were choosing a wedding date.) She agreed, and we consulted the senior partner, Arthur I. Vorys, to work it out. Arthur was immediately supportive, even though he was a dyed-in-the-wool Republican, because he understood the virtues of such involvement. I took the next three months off, unpaid, to work full-time on the campaign. I did not stop to consider my future as a lawyer or whether that would harm my career. Maybe I should have, but everything was moving so fast there just was not time.

Fortunately, Sue was an excellent mentor and very understanding, as was Arthur Vorys. Sue was a trailblazer as a lawyer. She was among the first female attorneys at our law firm and eventually became head of our Litigation Group. She served after law school as a law clerk to US District Judge Robert M. Duncan, a highly distinguished and experienced jurist and the first Black federal judge in Central Ohio. Sue is a sharp thinker and a tough negotiator with an even temperament. Having her on my side made me confident I was making a good choice. She saw the potential benefits for the firm, recognizing the positive recognition leadership of a successful campaign could bring. It was also only for a few months, so she supported my decision.

An unintended consequence of the campaign experience was the insight it gave me into the environment in which our state court judges operate. In Ohio, state court judges are elected by the voters, so it is incumbent upon the judges and judicial candidates to go through the political process. That means they need to win an election every six years, which involves campaigning, fundraising, engaging in general political activity, and keeping in touch with public opinion on an ongoing basis. At the same time, judges have an obligation to render judgment in the cases before them according to the law, without fear or favor and regardless of public opinion. That is a perilous tightrope to walk. The campaign experience gave me a better grasp of the judges' lives and careers.

I also learned a great deal about people and processes during my political campaigning, much of which was helpful to my law practice. Among the key lessons were the importance of details and the power of a compelling theme or narrative. Both are indispensable in a legal case. A lawyer needs to clearly define the client to the judge or jury and ensure the decision-makers appreciate the point of the case. Developing the essence of such a narrative is not easy; it requires a lot of pushing, pulling, and refining, but eventually, the irreducible essence emerges. These skills, honed through political campaigning, are applicable far beyond.

In the end, although Gary Hart won the Ohio primary in 1984, the campaign fell short at the Democratic National Convention in San Francisco that year. Former Vice President Mondale won the Democratic nomination but then lost to incumbent Ronald Reagan in the general election. Still, it felt like a triumph at the convention. Senator Hart gave an inspiring address, as did Nebraska Governor J. Robert Kerrey and Senator Christopher J. Dodd from Connecticut on his behalf. As "Chariots of Fire" by Vangelis played in the background after their speeches, a reporter for *The Youngstown Vindicator* asked how I felt. I stood beside him, too choked up to answer.

In the meantime, Senator Hart sent a letter of thanks during the summer after the convention. He reaffirmed that "a new generation of leadership has been introduced into American politics and, as I said in my speech at the Convention, someday will prevail." He was kind enough to add an overly generous handwritten postscript, of which I felt unworthy: "You were simply great, John. The best of the best." I could take such a compliment only as a tribute to the team of resourceful and energetic Ohio Democrats who together had brought his candidacy to the floor of the 1984 Democratic National Convention due to his victory in the Ohio primary.

I had many conversations with Senator Hart over the course of the effort I ran for him in Ohio that year and leading up to the campaign for the 1988 Democratic nomination. One particular conversation left a lasting impression. It was a Sunday in February 1987. We were in a car driving through Cleveland. There was a lot of fresh snow on the streets, causing the car to slide around. Senator Hart had just returned from a long trip to Moscow, where he had spent three days in meetings with Mikhail S. Gorbachev, the Communist Party leader of the Soviet Union at the time. General Secretary Gorbachev was in the process of introducing new political and economic freedoms in the Soviet Union—reforms that later led to the breakup of the USSR and Eastern Bloc and the reunification of

Germany and that gave the United States an opening for a new relationship with Russia.

Senator Hart talked at length about those conversations and the opportunities he could foresee. Listening to him articulate his outlook on the world, our national interests, and his strategies to serve those interests was a genuine inspiration. We had many other conversations over the years, but that particular one has always stood out to me; it epitomized why I was so zealous and excited to work for him. He had exactly the judgment and perspective I believed a good *president* should have.

Working with Senator Hart also reinforced my views about the importance of direct, person-to-person contact in a political campaign. Being able to speak directly with people, no matter the type of campaign, is an immensely valuable and fundamentally healthy way to learn and persuade. Senator Hart was proactive in reaching out to one voter at a time and building a new constituency for change within the Democratic Party, aiming to unite people around a common vision. He excelled at challenging established assumptions and the establishment itself. It was exhilarating to be part of that effort, and it affirmed my confidence in his approach to politics and governing.

Senator Hart *would* have made an excellent president, in my opinion, but he never got the chance. The subsequent 1988 campaign proved to be a sequel that ended in disappointment. In May 1987, after an intensive stakeout by several reporters who had been given a tip, the *Miami Herald* reported that a woman who was not his wife was spending a weekend at Senator Hart's condominium in Washington. By contrast, that was around the time thirty-seven US sailors lost their lives after a guided missile attack on a Navy ship in the Strait of Hormuz, and the United States began to provide naval coverage of oil tanker traffic in that highly charged region—an event far more transformative and important to our national interest but far less covered.

The sensationalized news of the suspected weekend guest completely undermined the campaign, forcing Senator Hart to withdraw within a week. In the perceptive words of journalist Matt Bai, it was "the very moment when the walls between public and private lives of candidates, between politics and celebrity, came tumbling down forever." In Bai's apt analysis, "Watergate, along with the deception over what was really happening in Vietnam, had injected into presidential politics a new focus on private morality." My comment to *The Plain Dealer* was "It's been a very hectic week with a very sad conclusion. Gary Hart has brought the Democratic Party to the brink of its future. Although that future will be lonelier without his candidacy, the dream that we share with him will live on."

I went to Denver for the withdrawal announcement, along with my Indiana counterpart Jack Wickes and dozens of other committed Hart supporters who had comprised the ongoing operation of the Hart campaign after 1984, to be with Senator Hart and his family. It was a sad day with a funereal overtone for all of us.

A few days later, Senator Hart called me at my apartment for a longer conversation than circumstances had allowed in Denver. I had just gotten back from the grocery store, where I impulsively bought a copy of the *National Enquirer* that featured on its cover a photograph of him and the woman in question aboard an unfortunately named boat (*Monkey Business*). The relationship, if any, did not really bother me, as I regarded that as purely their own business and Mrs. Hart's. I was more perplexed as to how there could be time for such relaxation while thousands of people were making many sacrifices for the benefit of the campaign. He was apologetic and urged me to remain active in politics and run for office myself. I thanked him for his confidence in me and urged him to always remember the distinctive opportunity his candidacy had given me and many other newcomers who had been able to help shape national politics and policy thanks to his leadership.

A few days after the end of the campaign, with plenty of time now on my hands, my colleagues at the law firm assigned me to go to Miami to help prepare for a large document production in a civil case. I stood on a downtown street corner on a sultry morning, waiting for the light to cross on my way to the offices to which I was headed. As I looked across the street, I saw, waiting on the other side, the *Miami Herald* reporter (suddenly a national figure after a steady flow of television interviews) whose story had toppled the Hart campaign. I got ready to give him a piece of my mind about what I thought of his work, which was such a deviation from the sounder journalistic discretion and judgment of the Ohio press corps. Rather than lose my temper, though, I let the opportunity slide by as we passed each other silently on the crosswalk.

Senator Hart had been the leading contender for the 1988 nomination. He was miles ahead of everybody else and looked to be the favorite. But he had picked up a lot of resistance from party insiders because he was never one of them. His candidacy presented a challenge to conventional wisdom, which is one of the things that appealed to me about him. After he stood down, Massachusetts Governor Michael S. Dukakis secured the nomination but eventually lost to Republican George H. W. Bush.

If Gary Hart had won the nomination and the presidency, I would have wanted to be part of the administration. I believe I understood him well. There were times during the campaign when I was giving speeches, and someone would ask his position on a certain issue. I knew intuitively what it would be, even if I had not read about it or looked it up. I would always check after the fact but was rarely wrong. I connected with his whole attitude and approach to international and domestic affairs, and I think he saw that. My career would have progressed differently had it not been for the abrupt end of his campaign.

Further Ohio Political Efforts

I have kept up my interest in political engagement over the years and stayed active in the Democratic Party. I began serving on the executive committee of the Franklin County Democratic Party in 1985. In 1986 I had the pleasure of managing the campaign of Herbert R. Brown, a talented trial lawyer at the Vorys firm, for the Supreme Court of Ohio. He ran in a contested primary, winning against a party-endorsed candidate, and went on to victory in the general election. His six years of service on the Supreme Court of Ohio were a matter of great pride to everyone who knew him.

Among the memorable vignettes of that campaign was an astute observation by Vicki Foley, whose husband Jim was a colleague at the law firm. Vicki had had little experience in politics. Watching the election returns with us on election night at the Ohio secretary of state's office, she noticed a twenty-thousand-vote aberration in the results for Herb Brown in one of the large urban counties compared to the pattern in the surrounding counties. We brought that to the attention of the secretary of state's team, and the unintentional error was corrected, putting Herb Brown in the lead.

It was just as satisfactory to help in 1992 with the election of Beverly Pfeiffer to the Common Pleas Court of Franklin County, Ohio. Beverly, an accomplished lawyer, and her husband Bill, whose uncommonly sound legal, political, and business judgment distinguish him, had been close friends of Maryline and mine for many years. Well before Franklin County turned into a Democratic stronghold, Beverly won the campaign by an impressive margin and was among the first Democratic women to serve as a trial judge locally.

While Maryline and I were in the thick of raising children, our political engagement necessarily took a back seat to familial and professional responsibilities. One function that was fun for the whole family, though, was a fundraising lunch we hosted at our home for Tipper Gore, the spouse of Vice President Al Gore, in the course of his bid for the White House in 2000. It was the first such fundraiser we had ever hosted, and we had to do so on short notice. Along the way I learned a lot about the fundraising process. Particularly meaningful was the support of the mental health community in Ohio, given Mrs. Gore's strong advocacy of mental health care and the servicing of mental health at a level of parity with other medical needs. She had served as mental health policy adviser to President Clinton and worked effectively to end the stigma then associated with mental illness. The fundraiser was quite successful, with attendance by a wide range of avid Democrats who vigorously supported the Gore campaign.

Also enjoyable was the role I got to play in heading up the debate preparation for Ohio gubernatorial candidate Ted Strickland, a Democratic member of Congress from southern Ohio who won the governor's office in 2006. I volunteered for the assignment after an impromptu opportunity to host Iowa Governor Thomas J. Vilsack, a Democrat, at the law firm one afternoon. I invited everyone from the firm who had any connection with Iowa to join us. The dialogue with Governor Vilsack that day reminded me how much I missed having a Democrat as governor of Ohio. I wanted to do what I could to help in the upcoming election with the experience I had gained from being a lawyer.

It was thoroughly refreshing to work with then-Congressman Strickland. In addition to handling the logistics of debate preparation and drafting the debate agreement with the Republican opponent, my main job was to anticipate and ask the questions that were likely to come up in the series of gubernatorial debates. That involved a systematic review of the major operations of the state government on my part, which was deeply interesting and worthwhile.

The most impressive things about Congressman Strickland were the sincerity and command of the issues he brought to the debate preparation exercises and the complete candor with which he addressed every question. He answered in a straightforward manner, without any hesitation or calculation of how to spin things. There was never an occasion when he said one thing in the privacy of the debate preparation room and another thing in public. He was consistent throughout.

As governor, Ted Strickland served the people of Ohio faithfully and well. We did the same sort of debate preparation in advance of the 2010 election, a campaign that fell short due to the severe economic havoc the Great Recession of 2008 had caused in Ohio and across the nation.

When Senator Barack H. Obama ran for president in 2008, any hope of involvement in the general election campaign on my part was lost when a judge put one of my major cases on a fast track and set the trial date for just after the election. In the last couple of weeks of the campaign, we were in the thick of the discovery and trial preparation phase of the litigation. It was a huge case, and it consumed all my time. For those who had been able to campaign, it was a truly historic win, with a lot of celebration down the street from the law firm, where we were working late into the night to prepare for the trial. During the primary election earlier that year, a law firm colleague and I, who each worked with the same secretary, had been amicably involved in coordinating the competing candidacy petitions of Senator Obama and Senator Hillary Clinton. We mused that, regardless of the outcome of the primary election, the one person who was sure to end up working in the White House was our secretary. Fortunately for the law firm, our longtime secretary stayed at the firm. Fortunately for the nation, my colleague became the US Attorney for the Southern District of Ohio.

Chapter 9:
Serving the Community and Learning the World

Perhaps because I came of age in the inspirational era of leaders like President Kennedy, Governor Gilligan, and Governor Celeste, community service focused on the common good has always seemed to me one of the worthiest callings for lawyers and all other citizens. In the forty-five years since I graduated from law school, it has become increasingly clear to me as a lawyer that civic responsibility is essential to good public service and requires, above all, respect for the community the leader is serving. Learning about the community through public service has, in turn, been a source of great satisfaction and professional understanding through those years.

Civic responsibility is—in my mind—like the responsibility a lawyer owes to judges and juries: to provide sufficient accurate information to be able to make the right decision. The same is true of responsibility to the voters. When going door to door in a campaign, I have found that most voters take the process seriously. When we are face-to-face on their doorstep, they are looking to me to listen to them and shed what light I can on issues they raise. I want to give them information that will be helpful to their decision in the election and their evaluation of the issues that are important to them. And always, because people are smart, they are much more receptive to talking if they understand I am being honest with them and talking about something that really matters. On the doorstep, and in public service generally, I regard myself as an officer of the voter and the community in the same way the lawyer is an officer of the court.

Political engagement is only one of the ways in which I have tried to serve the community as a lawyer. Respect for the importance of community service is one of the main reasons I accepted the job offer from my law firm over forty years ago. There seemed to be more people there than at any other Ohio law firm who were actively involved in community leadership. It is healthy for the individual, a benefit to the firm, and good for the community.

The Columbus Zoo

When I went to Africa in 1980, my intention was to learn about its legal and political structures. Because I was seeing the continent on such a low budget, I was hitching lifts in cars and on the backs of trucks, staying in youth hostels and cheap hotels, and experiencing Africa on the ground. That brought me into close proximity with the continent's wildlife. Seeing the animals in their natural habitats made it clear to me that this is as much their world as it is ours.

After I got home, I applied to serve on the board of trustees of the Columbus Zoo in order to have more opportunities for encounters with wildlife. I ended up serving on the zoo board for thirty-four years, initially as a board member and eventually as president and chair of the board. All of that stemmed from seeing animals on the savanna in Africa from the backs of dusty trucks and on paths through the bush.

Everything I did as a zoo board member was on a volunteer basis. It generally took about five hours a week, except when I served as board president, when it became more like fifteen to twenty hours a week. The law firm was supportive, provided I also kept up my responsibilities to the firm and our clients. I had to fit these activities into my "spare" time. Thankfully, my career has taught me to make the most of those "extra" hours.

When I joined the board in 1982, it was a different zoo than it is today. It was still a relatively small municipal park on the outskirts of town, founded in 1927 on excess land owned by the City of Columbus for water supply management. It had had several exciting moments, including the birth of the first gorilla in captivity in 1956. But it was lacking in funding and almost entirely dependent on the City of Columbus to meet its budget, and most of the animals were housed in small cages. A new day was coming, though, under the inspired leadership of Jack Hanna, who became zoo director in 1978. Jack was determined to take the Columbus Zoo to a whole new level. Through enthusiasm, resourcefulness, and a thoroughly charismatic personality, he and Columbus Recreation and Parks Director Melvin B. Dodge were able to start the gradual expansion of the Columbus Zoo into the monumental institution it has become today. Jack Hanna had a dream, and he turned that dream into a reality.

One of the main ways I was able to help was by assisting in the effort to win adoption of a countywide zoo levy by the Franklin County voters. A domestic relations judge from Toledo, Ohio, shared with me the legal documentation necessary to put a zoo levy on the ballot under Ohio law. Along with others on behalf of the Columbus Zoological Park Association, I worked with city and county officials to lay the legal groundwork for the first levy in 1985 and ran the campaign to win voter approval. The campaign was successful. The first zoo levy went into effect shortly afterward, spreading the tax burden and giving the Columbus Zoo a steady and modestly increased revenue stream from which to serve the public.

I remained involved with subsequent levy proposals, which the Franklin County voters adopted in 1990, 1994, 2004, and 2015 (plus one for a proposal, originated by others, which the voters rejected in 2014). In the process, along with dramatically increased visitation and philanthropy, the annual budget of the Columbus Zoo grew from $3.2 million when I started in 1982 to over $61 million when I left the board in 2016.

Adoption of the zoo levy led to the arrival of Jerry Borin at the Columbus Zoo, first as executive director and eventually as director and president. Jerry Borin is one of the finest public administrators with whom I have ever had the privilege of working. His even temperament, conscientious focus, and unflinching dedication to public service allowed the Columbus Zoo to flourish under his leadership. In his engagement with zoo board members and the deeply passionate team of zoo employees, Jerry was equally effective because of the humility with which he views himself and the respect he consistently shows for others. Authority naturally flowed to him and allowed him to steadily lead the Columbus Zoo into the new era Jack Hanna and Mel Dodge had ushered in.

The Franklin County levy, alongside substantial private fundraising efforts, has made a major difference in the ability of the Columbus Zoo to protect and preserve its animal collection and serve the educational and recreational interests of the public. Among its conservation priorities was the creation of an outdoor facility that has given many of the African animal species at the zoo substantial room to roam. I had seen in Africa how beautiful and free the animals are in their natural habitats, which gave me an incentive to replicate that environment, to the extent possible, at the Columbus Zoo.

It was a long process to create the Heart of Africa exhibit. I was delighted to play a small, supportive part. First, there needed to be a large enough site to make the exhibit feasible. An opportunity became available for Franklin County and the City of Columbus to acquire a huge tract of land adjacent to the Columbus Zoo, which would otherwise be gone forever if others developed it into residential and commercial usages. The land was bought with the benefit of a three-way arrangement between the Columbus Zoological Park Association, Franklin County, and the City of Columbus. The next challenge was getting the Heart of Africa exhibit into the zoo's capital plan. Even after the land was secured, it was quite an expensive project. At that point, the focus turned to a combination of tax levy proceeds and private fundraising.

In tandem with the Heart of Africa initiative on the zoo grounds in suburban Columbus, the zoo also took over operation of a more remote, separate ten-thousand-acre facility called the Wilds, near Zanesville, Ohio, about one hundred miles away from the zoo. The acreage (reclaimed strip-mine land) is dedicated to wildlife conservation, allowing animals the space to roam. They can run in herds, climb trees, wallow in water holes, and behave as they would on the savanna. One of the most wonderful things is watching people watch the animals. Sitting there is almost like going out with the guide in Zimbabwe; the scale is vast, and rhinos, zebras, and other species saunter by in their element.

Over the course of my thirty-four years as a board member, the agendas of our monthly board meetings covered a lot of ground. In addition to routine business, we dealt with arrangements with China for a loan of pandas to the Columbus Zoo in 1992. The secretary of education of the United States came to one of our meetings in 1997 to highlight the exceptional education programs of the Columbus Zoo. We were proud to develop a strong relationship with several programs in Rwanda, personified by a young man named Frederick Ndabaramiye, whose hands were hacked off during the genocide when he refused to kill people but who survived to become a leader of his community and an inspiration to us all. My litigation experience in accounting and auditing cases proved useful when we received the annual report of the outside auditors, to whom I would pose a standard series of questions designed to probe their conclusions. All the while, the Columbus Zoo continued its steady growth to become one of the leading zoos in the nation.

When the zoo opened a new lion exhibit in 1997, I had to find a guest speaker for the ribbon-cutting ceremony. I turned to the senior federal judge in the nation, Joseph P. Kinneary, who was serving on the United States District Court for the Southern District of Ohio in Columbus. His Honor had literally growled at me during my first jury trial in federal court in the 1980s, a terrifying and unforgettable moment, when I asked him to reconsider his ruling on an important evidentiary objection. Because he had figuratively been a lion of the law in the courtroom that day, he was a natural choice for the opening of the lion exhibit. At age ninety-one, he rose to the occasion that afternoon, reminding my fellow trustees and me, as we listened spellbound, that "nothing is more important than responsibility. Responsibility is what gives us a reason to live every day. You must never forget your responsibility."

One zoo leader who posthumously taught me an equally valuable lesson was the late Jeff Swanagan. We first met when he came for an interview to be the zoo director. The minute he walked into the room, it was obvious he was the person we should choose. He was born to be a zoo director—a man whose talent, temperament, and experience fitted him perfectly for the position. He took the job and got off to a strong start. But out of the blue, he had a heart attack and died in the summer of 2009 while cutting his grass. It was a real shock.

There was a memorial service for him at the zoo, and his stepdaughter was planning to speak about him. I worked with her beforehand, helping her organize her thoughts about what she was going to say. Among other things, I asked questions to help her, such as when she first met him. She said his genuine enthusiasm for animals, conservation, and zoos stood out when she started to get to know Jeff. Prompted by how much he loved his vocation, she had asked him, "How did you know what to do with your life?" He responded, "It's easy. You just find what you love and *make* it your life." Jeff Swanagan personified that advice because he himself had found what he loved and made it his life. It is easy to tell when we are with people like that. When someone is said to have charisma, it is usually because the person has found what they love and can make it their life. When I heard that story, it reminded me of the way I had felt when sitting in the courtyard before my first day at Yale Law School, knowing that was going to be forever.

These are some of the many lessons I learned by virtue of serving on the Columbus Zoo board of trustees. Above all, as I had seen in Africa, this is not just our world. It is also the world of every other living creature, on the land, in the water, and above us in the sky. The Scriptures remind us that we are the stewards of this creation and have a responsibility to treat our world with respect—a responsibility it was an honor to help discharge with the Columbus Zoo.

Ohio History

History, as one of my other chief interests, has motivated several efforts I have made on behalf of the community. With ongoing gratitude for the moon rocks that saved the day for me as a high school chemistry student over twenty-five years earlier, I eagerly took the opportunity to run for election to the board of trustees of the Ohio Historical Society and served on the board for nine years, beginning in 1996. It was a fascinating role; the organization is charged with the preservation and protection of Ohio history. In addition to the artifacts in its collection, its archives include a wide range of materials, from memoirs of private individuals to document collections of former public officials. I got my initial exposure to the archives while in college, finding them to be a valuable primary source for research papers as a history major. The archives became increasingly impressive to me as I learned more about them during the nine years I served on the board.

As a board member, and also as a member of the Ohio Bicentennial Commission, one of my main objectives was to raise the profile of Ohio historical sites and make them more attractive and accessible. One good example is the Rankin House, which sits on a hill overlooking the Ohio River in southwestern Ohio. Built in 1825, it was owned by Reverend John Rankin, a Presbyterian minister and abolitionist. Across the river is Kentucky, which, before the Civil War, was a slave state. Slavery had been forbidden in Ohio since the adoption of the Northwest Ordinance in 1787, a prohibition the Ohio Constitution reiterated when Ohio entered the Union. But because of the Fugitive Slave Law of 1850, runaway slaves were still subject to arrest in Ohio, so they needed safe, undetected passage to get them out of the country and into Canada. Reverend Rankin would light a lantern in a specific window when it was safe for fleeing slaves to cross the river and then hide them in a concealed cellar until they could continue onward on the Underground Railroad—as the clandestine route to Canada was called—and to freedom. The lantern that shone from his home was a beacon for freedom then and now.

I loved my involvement with the Ohio Historical Society. A few years after I began my board service, Maryline was talking with one of the society's division heads whom I had not seen for a while. He asked Maryline how I enjoyed the responsibilities. Using a colloquial expression to tell him how happy I was, Maryline said, "Oh, he's just died and gone to heaven!" The division head took her literally, and bowed and said, "Oh, I'm so sorry, I hadn't heard." Maryline cleared up the ambiguity, and they both had a good laugh about that. But the metaphorical point was right. It was an honor to serve on the Ohio Historical Society board for three terms and promote the preservation of Ohio's history in that way.

One of the most educational and fascinating projects I undertook outside the board service was the preparation of a written history of the Ohio governor's office. Along with several other history-minded lawyers and professors, I took part in authorship of the two-volume book called *The History of Ohio Law*, published by the Ohio University Press on the occasion of the bicentennial of Ohio statehood in 2003. My assignment was the chapter on how the constitutional and statutory powers and responsibilities of the Ohio governor have evolved.

The starting point was a strong territorial governor during the Northwest Territory era, leading up to Ohio's formal admission to the Union in 1803. Reacting to perceived abuse of that power, the first Ohio Constitution made the governor a mere figurehead, with little vested authority. That changed over time: Voters adopted the second Ohio Constitution in 1851, restoring various powers to the governor, and the legislature made significant additions to the governor's appointment power and executive responsibilities. Adoption of veto power in the early twentieth century made the governor a significant participant in the legislative process. By the dawn of the twenty-first century, the constitution and laws of the state of Ohio enabled the governor to wield substantial authority—hence the title of the chapter I contributed, "Reinventing the Governor: A History of Executive Power Under Ohio Law."

In preparing the chapter on gubernatorial power, I had the enjoyable opportunity to read the entire compilation of annual State of the State messages delivered by Ohio's governors to the General Assembly. The compilation is available at the State Library of Ohio. It provides the reader with a brilliant overview of Ohio history since the early days of statehood and, with its consecutive recounting of the many challenges the state has overcome, a strong basis for optimism about the future of Ohio.

Catholic Diocese of Columbus

I also had the honor of serving on the board of Catholic Social Services of the Diocese of Columbus for seven years, including several years as president and chair. Under the auspices of Catholic Social Services, thousands of people in central and southern Ohio are able to have more dignity in their lives and additional support for their basic human needs. I have never seen an organization that could squeeze as much out of a nickel as Catholic Social Services, using the limited resources at its disposal to further the social doctrine prescribed by Pope Leo XIII in his 1891 encyclical *Rerum Novarum* and reiterated by Pope John Paul II in his encyclical *Centesimus Annus* a century later, both of which applied the teachings of Jesus to the conditions of the industrial era.

A more somber responsibility came my way for ten years as a member of the Board of Review for the Protection of Children, including six years as chair. It was the job of the board to make a prompt initial assessment of the credibility of allegations of sexual abuse by priests, deacons, and other church personnel and present recommendations for action by the bishop. The board took its responsibility seriously and carried it out with heavy hearts. No other form of community service left me so sad.

As a Catholic, my faith has never wavered, even though my own observance of Catholic doctrines and practices has hardly been faultless over the years, with occasional lapses that leave me as dependent upon the promise of redemption and forgiveness of sin as I have been from the beginning.

Learning the World Through My Feet

Learning the world through my feet, to use the phrase coined by my Israeli travel companions in Africa, became an integral part of my life once I had the experience of traveling after law school. After nearly every trip, I have returned home with more respect for cultural differences and a better definition of myself by comparison with the people I met.

For a short journey in 1981, several months after I started at the law firm, I flew to Mexico City and went by bus down through Mexico, Guatemala, Honduras, El Salvador, and Nicaragua. It was another low-budget foray, which maximized the time I could spend on the ground with the people and their day-to-day activities, including a roadside meal at daybreak in eastern Guatemala after an all-night bus ride and a lively patriotic concert one evening in Managua, where the Sandinista revolutionaries had recently overthrown the government of Nicaragua.

Two years later I went to Israel, Jordan, and Syria. Every moment of a trip to the Middle East is inherently fascinating, given the unique density of religious, cultural, historical, and political features. In Jerusalem I stayed at the YMCA and saw many parts of Israel while based there. The trips to Amman in Jordan and Damascus in Syria gave me an improved understanding of the complex geography and politics of that part of the Middle East.

With Maryline, I went back to Israel in September 2012. I saw a nation that seemed more secure and had grown considerably in the nearly three decades since I first visited. But I was saddened to also see the vast proliferation of walls that had come to dominate the landscape in many areas. Maryline and I were in Israel around the time of the attacks against two US government posts in Benghazi, Libya, which culminated in the deaths of the US ambassador and a Foreign Service officer. Protests quickly spread throughout North Africa.

The regional tensions made us especially vigilant during a nighttime ride through the occupied West Bank on the way to the Sea of Galilee. We departed Jerusalem by car at two in the morning to arrive on time at the starting point for the fifty-ninth annual Sea of Galilee swim, the largest amateur sports event in Israel. Our transit was uneventful, including at the border checkpoints, and the event was superb as I swam through waters that were brimming with religious and historical meaning. Events in the Middle East since then have underscored the good fortune of having had the peaceful interlude for that swim.

In 1986 I went to India on a trip organized by the Rotary Club. The global purpose of the Rotary organization is to serve others and promote peace through fellowship of business, professional, and community leaders. Over time, Rotary's reach and vision have gradually extended to include humanitarian services. Members have a long track record of effectively addressing challenges in their communities and around the world.

One day in 1985, I saw a story in *The Columbus Dispatch* that the local Rotary Club was holding a competition to select individuals for a group study exchange trip to India. The presiding partner of the law firm, John Elam, allowed me to pursue the opportunity, so I completed the application and submitted it. One debt I owe is to former US Secretary of State Kissinger, whom I met briefly around that time after he gave a speech at The Ohio State University. I asked Secretary Kissinger what formed his worldview about India, and he immediately said it was important to remember India is the world's largest democracy. His observation was an important talking point in my interview with the Rotary Club selection committee.

The Rotarians selected me and four other young men from central Ohio. Everyone in the group was in his late twenties or early thirties. All of us were single with no children. None of us were Rotary Club members, as Rotarians were ineligible due to legal requirements.

It was a six-week trip through the state of Uttar Pradesh in the north of India, the most populous state (with nearly 200 million people at present). We stayed in the homes of Indian Rotarians, visited their places of employment and their children's schools by day, and attended Rotary Club meetings at which we spoke many evenings. It was a fascinating way to see India because we were off the tourist track, visiting lesser-known towns such as Bareilly, Shahjahanpur, and Lucknow as well as the Taj Mahal at Agra. It gave us spectacular exposure to day-to-day India.

I looked forward to the speeches at the local Rotary Club meetings. It was essentially the same speech every time, with an interpreter usually translating our words into Hindi. I gradually learned how to deliver at least the first part of the speech in Hindi. The difference it made was astounding. The first night I opened the speech in Hindi, there was instant applause, even after the first sentence. The people in the audience were so excited to hear an effort to speak in their native tongue. In doing so, I had been inspired by Pope John Paul II when I saw how effective it was for him to be able to communicate the message he wanted to deliver by speaking in the language of the local audiences with whom he visited around the world.

One other language lesson I learned in India was the importance of a common national language. The people of India (now 1.35 billion) do not share the same language. Hindi is the predominant language, along with English. But other languages, including Bengali, Marathi, Telegu, Tamil, and over 120 others, are widespread as well. The result, which we saw firsthand, is that people in one part of India often cannot talk with people from another part about matters of common national interest. It struck me that democracy is complicated enough as it is, and the inability to communicate directly with each other is a substantial impediment that nations should strive to avoid.

The US space shuttle *Challenger* exploded during our trip. It was a national tragedy back home and a sad moment for all of us on the trip. I listened to the news in several languages on a shortwave radio I had bought in India, even though the only word I recognized in many broadcasts was "*Challenger*." It might have been American news, but the impact was global.

While we were there, we also got to see the range and scope of the service work the Rotary Club undertakes all around the world. The hospitals and clinics we visited were sponsored by Rotary. Hundreds of people would be there waiting to see a physician. The medical care they received was impressive.

I was grateful to the Rotary Club from the moment we landed in India, on New Year's Day 1986, for such a unique journey. My teammates and I experienced the warm hospitality of our Indian family hosts throughout Uttar Pradesh. We traveled daily in the colorful but harrowing procession of buses, trucks, cars, bicycles, elephants, cattle, and pedestrians along the busy streets and highways. We became acquainted with new foods and cultures. We visited teeming industrial factories and busy carpet looms. We saw and learned about the businesses in which the Rotarians were engaged. We drove through vast fields of yellow mustard plants and brilliant green farmlands. We saw the contrast between elegant opulence and stark poverty. Every day was a great adventure, from which we learned a lot.

In an ongoing effort to learn the world through my feet, I have tried to meet people and visit communities in a wide range of other places. In the spring of 1987, a twin-engine propeller plane took me and several others from Resolute, in the north of Canada, up to Lake Hazen and then to a landing at the North Pole, a frozen icecap atop the Arctic Ocean. (Early spring is the only time that is possible because the sun has risen sufficiently above the horizon to provide enough light to see but not enough warmth to melt the thick ice on which the plane lands.) Most impressive to me was the extent and strategic significance of the Arctic region, which had come to my attention during the Gary Hart campaign, and the dangerous beauty of its icy landscape.

Maryline and I were members of a June 1989 delegation of the American Council of Young Political Leaders on a trip to Hungary, which was emerging from decades of communist rule, and Poland, which was in the midst of its first free elections in modern times. Maryline was seven months pregnant, leading some to wonder whether our delegation would be larger on the way home than when we got there. Our group met daily with political leaders of all parties. In Poland it was clear the Solidarity Party had stirred great support, and the communist-affiliated parties faced the once unimaginable prospect of losing power. Unforgettable to both of us was the genuine excitement and gleam in people's eyes on the streets of Warsaw and Kraków and many small towns as they prepared to vote.

Maryline and I pose for a photo while visiting the headquarters of the Solidarity Party in Warsaw, Poland, June 1989.

I had a first-time experience in Warsaw while waiting one day in a hotel for an international phone line I had reserved to make a call back to the United States. When the line was ready, the receptionist paged me. I went to the window and told her who I was. Another gentleman standing there said, "No, that's me." It turned out his surname was Hulewicz, and he had slightly misheard the announcement. It was an amusing moment for me, having never imagined anyone outside my immediate family would have a similar-sounding last name.

Along the same line, a Connecticut lawyer named Harvey J. Kulawitz wrote me a lighthearted letter seven years later, insisting I "immediately cease and desist" from using his last name. He mentioned a Connecticut Superior Court judge "who also bears a name similar to ours"—Judge Joanne Kiely Kulawiz of Milford. By coincidence, Judge Kulawiz had written to me a few years earlier after reading a newspaper story about a case I had handled. She helpfully explained that "because of the use of the Cyrillic alphabet" in the region from which many people with surnames like ours had emigrated, "the spelling of the name has taken many forms" when it was translated from their passports. Indeed, an immigration officer at Ellis Island is believed to have translated my paternal grandfather's surname as "Kuliewicz" from the Cyrillic script of the authorities who had issued his passport. That is the spelling he used for the rest of his life.

The pronunciation of the name has evolved over time. Rendered in the old country as "koo-LEV-ich," it is now articulated here as "COOL-uh-wits." One of my newer colleagues at the law firm thought the articulation had evolved further when there was a page one day over the intercom for John Kuhl ("cool"), a partner whom she did not yet know. She mistakenly assumed the operator had paged me with a shortened form of my last name meant as a sort of caricature.

Chapter 10:
Upper Arlington City Council

The call to community service led me to run successfully for public office—the City Council of Upper Arlington, Ohio—for the first time in 2019, and for reelection four years later in 2023. The focus of each campaign was door-to-door, direct conversations with my fellow residents (a local version of learning the world through my feet). One sunny afternoon during the second campaign, as I was walking up to a home on Cheshire Road for such a conversation, a young boy and his friends were gathering on the driveway for a bike ride. Before they left, the boy's father said to them, "Make good decisions." He was right, not just for his son but for all who serve the community in any capacity. I have adopted his advice as a good reminder of what the community expects of any public official.

Upper Arlington Today

Maryline and I have lived in Upper Arlington since 1987 and have seen great change in the years since then. Development of the community began in 1916, after a slight delay for use of a large tract for training eight thousand members of the Ohio National Guard for deployment to Mexico to hunt down General Francisco "Pancho" Villa. Upper Arlington was incorporated as a village in 1918 and as a city in 1941, then adopted a city charter in 1956. From the outset, the city has been a relatively prosperous part of the Columbus area. The median income today is approximately $125,000, compared to the state of Ohio average of $60,000, and the median home value is nearly $450,000. Its public schools are among the highest ranked in the state. Educational attainment also is high, with over 78 percent of the adult population having earned a bachelor's degree or above.

As with other communities, though, resources are not necessarily spread evenly. Several hundred students in the Upper Arlington school system receive free or reduced-price lunches, nearly one thousand residents live at or below the poverty line, community volunteers pack grocery bags with meals for food-insecure families in our neighborhoods, and the Upper Arlington Community Foundation often lends a hand to those in temporary need. Restrictive deed covenants prohibited Black ownership of certain real estate until the Supreme Court of the United States rendered that practice, widespread across the nation, unenforceable in 1948. The demographic composition of the city has changed gradually since then. Today the suburb is making a deliberate effort to welcome and include people of all races.

Politically, the city has changed enormously over the decades. In 1956 President Dwight D. Eisenhower, a Republican, won 88 percent of the Upper Arlington vote in his successful bid for reelection, leaving Democratic presidential nominee Adlai Stevenson with only 12 percent. Likewise, in 1960, the city voted 82 percent for Republican Richard M. Nixon and 18 percent for Democrat John F. Kennedy. The results began to become more even by the 2008 election. By 2020 Democrat Joseph R. Biden Jr. won 63.7 percent of the vote in Upper Arlington, against Republican President Donald J. Trump. In 2024 Vice President Kamala D. Harris, a Democrat, won every precinct, with a total of 62.25 percent of the vote, with 35.9 percent for former President Trump. The suburbanization of the Democratic Party has manifested itself dramatically at the voting booth in Upper Arlington.

How the Upper Arlington Pools Changed My Life

My decision to run for city council was prompted by a debt I have owed the UA pools since July 5, 2001. I remember the day because I woke up that morning feeling wiped out from the day before—the Fourth of July, which is a big deal in Upper Arlington. It is a daylong event, starting at the time with early morning megaphone wake-up announcements from roving cars, followed by a morning-long parade, neighborhood block parties, and cookouts, and then a major fireworks display as soon as it becomes dark. It is exhausting, especially when you have young children. When I got out of bed the next morning, feeling the need to do something to shake off the feeling of lethargy, I remembered I had read about an "Early Bird Swim" at the Tremont Pool in Upper Arlington. With low expectations, I decided to check it out.

Early summer mornings are the best time of the year in Ohio. The sun rises early, the air is fresh, the skies are usually clear, and the birds are singing. In my memory, at least, it was a morning like that on July 5, 2001. The Early Bird Swim opened at six thirty at the Tremont Pool, which is one of the three outdoor public pools operated by the City of Upper Arlington. A handful of people were there. I found an empty lane and got in. I had to stop after every lap (round trip) to catch my breath but felt better after finishing and decided to come back. After a few more days with the same stop-and-start sequence but a good feeling afterward, I made it my goal to swim ten laps (twenty lengths of the twenty-five-yard pool) without stopping by the end of the summer.

I went back day after day, and some days, it was grueling. In those first few hundred yards, I would think, *I'm tired, I ache*, or, *It would be so much nicer to be sleeping or drinking coffee and reading the newspaper*. I would question why I was putting myself through such exertion. But then—all of a sudden—I would get through the proverbial wall and settle into the swim. As an added bonus, swimming started to make me feel healthier, especially after sedentary years spent mostly behind a desk at the office and driving in carpools from one school event to another. The hardest part is putting on your swimsuit, as is sometimes said.

While I was at the pool, I started to meet and talk with other swimmers my age and found a congenial and appealing group of people whom I liked a lot. Plus, I admired the groups of men and women in their eighties who came to the pool every day, many by bike, to swim laps. They all seemed cheerful and strong, which was a real inspiration, as it started to dawn upon me there was a risk I might live that long someday.

The path on which I started at the UA pools in the summer of 2001 has led to swimming adventures around the world and turned swimming into a hugely positive part of my life. The adventures started with pool races in Ohio and then evolved into open-water swims of increasingly longer distances and greater challenges. It felt as if my life had gained a new dimension.

The first open-water swim prompted by my experience in the UA pools was a 1-mile crossing of the Columbia River, from Washington State to Oregon, in the 2009 annual Labor Day swim at Hood River. Two years later, I swam in the 3.2-mile annual crossing of the Hellespont, also known as the Dardanelles, in Turkey, made famous by Lord Byron in 1810. Along with hundreds of other swimmers from around the world, I made it across from the Gallipoli peninsula, on the European side, to Çanakkale on the Asian side.

Then there was a 13.7-mile swim across the Strait of Gibraltar, between Spain and Morocco, in 2013, an exciting way to return to Africa for the first time since my journey after law school. The swim required months of preparation in a series of increasingly long and challenging open-water swims. As I neared the African coast, the melody and words of the African anthem *"Mungu ibariki Afrika"* played in my mind, reminding me of when I had first heard the hymn almost thirty-three years before, far above sea level on the slopes of Mount Kilimanjaro.

Thanks to my team, I was oblivious to the ships while swimming across the Strait of Gibraltar, October 2013.

With inspiration likewise derived from swimming in the UA pools, I also organized and served as captain of three English Channel relay teams. The commemorative purposes of the English Channel relays made our landings in France quite emotional. The team announcement I sent after we reached the French shore for the D-Day anniversary swim bespoke those sentiments: "In grateful memory of those who won a victory for freedom on D-Day 1944, the Overlord 70 relay swim team crossed the Channel from England to France today in twelve hours and eight minutes. May God bless those to whom we all owe so much." The return to the English Channel, which I had first seen during the Oxford program over forty years earlier, made each of the relay swims even more meaningful to me.

The Overlord 70 team on June 8, 2014, at the White Horse Inn in Dover, where swimmers customarily go after a successful crossing of the English Channel to sign the wall or ceiling. From left to right: Kevin Murphy (our official observer and honorary secretary of the Channel Swimming & Piloting Federation, the accrediting body), me, Joe Hall, John Boyd, Edward Williams, Bryan Avery, and James Penrose.

The Over There! relay team in June 2017, on the beach at Dover Harbor after swimming through the night across the English Channel in honor of the one hundredth anniversary of the arrival of US troops in France for World War I. The French swimmers are (from left to right) Alexandre Fleury, William Bonnet, Philippe Fort, Nicolas Costa, and (sixth and seventh from the left) Nicolas Derrien and Eve Gaillard. The American swimmers are Michelle Dean Sanders (fifth from left) and (starting eighth from left) John Stephan, me, James Curphey, David Arnold, and Richard Lovering.

With ongoing encouragement from UA pool swimming, I also completed a 4-mile downstream crossing of the Bosphorus in Istanbul in 2015. Three years later, on the seventy-fifth anniversary of the sinking of PT 109, I led a team to the Solomon Islands to swim the 4.2-mile route President Kennedy and the survivors had taken after a Japanese destroyer sank their vessel in 1943. The tribute to JFK and the PT 109 crew was especially poignant for those of us whose fathers and uncles had served in the American forces in the Pacific Theater during World War II. Most recent was a 2-mile swim across the Strait of Messina, from Sicily to the Italian mainland in 2024. I hope there will be more to come.

I am forever grateful to the Upper Arlington pools where these adventures all originated with the Early Bird Swim at the Tremont Pool in 2001. I have learned two main lessons from these swimming experiences, thanks to the UA pools. First is the importance, in any such team effort, of finding swimmers who are faster, stronger, and even more durable than me to maximize our chance of success—a lesson readily applicable to any team-building exercise. A swimmer encounters many obstacles in such swims—jellyfish, cold water, strong currents, tides, debris, rough water, and other challenges—that would make it easy to quit. The important thing is to swim through them. Push the demons aside. Acclimatize to the cold. When stung by a jellyfish, defy the culprit: "Is that the best you can do? Is that all you've got?" Through it all, just keep swimming. Teammates with more talent and experience than I have are especially valuable under such conditions.

I am no less grateful to the UA pools for what these swims have taught me about the power of dreams and imagination. I have no particular gifts as a swimmer and little to show for my swimming by way of record-setting times or distances. But I have a decent imagination. When the ideas of these swims have caught my mind, I have figured out a way to do them. The training has been intense, and the demands upon my mental fortitude have been enormous. But imagination has proved to be a powerful force in transforming desire into accomplishment.

Running for City Council

Expressing my gratitude through service on the Upper Arlington City Council came about due to a swimming experience on Labor Day weekend in 2018. I earlier had trained and qualified for American Red Cross lifeguard certification because of my open-water swimming activities, to be better equipped to help if something went wrong out in the ocean with any of my teammates. A few weeks before Labor Day weekend, when I was leaving the city pool after a daily swim, I saw a sign that said the pool was going to close over the Labor Day holiday because there were not enough lifeguards (the college and high school students who normally comprise the lifeguard corps having almost all gone back to school by that point). The notice also asked for volunteers.

I signed up to serve as a lifeguard, as did several other adults. It became possible to keep the pool open, and hundreds of people came that Labor Day weekend. It was a beautiful weekend, and it was inspiring to know that, because the lifeguards were there, the city was able to open the pools—and families from throughout the community were having a great time. I loved the responsibility of being there on the deck, protecting the people in the water and ensuring everyone was safe.

That got me thinking about other potential opportunities for public service. I was at a stage in my career when I needed to start thinking about what would come next—what to do after my upcoming mandatory departure from the law firm partnership at the end of 2024, the year in which I would turn seventy, which was then faintly on the horizon. Because I loved the three public pools in Upper Arlington so much, serving on the city council was one possible option; it would support the important service the pools provide to the thirty-seven thousand residents of the city. At first, running for city council did not seem like a constructive thing to do. The City of Upper Arlington already was moving in the right direction, as far as I was concerned. It would not make much sense to displace an incumbent when things were going so well. But then one of the incumbents, Susan M. Ralph, announced she had decided not to seek reelection.

Shortly after I heard about the vacancy, I threw my hat in the ring. My family was supportive because they knew what a positive difference the UA pools had made for me and many others and how important public service was to each of us. I met individually with the other city council members and community members from various neighborhoods and walks of life and started inquiring about what a local campaign would involve. I was encouraged by everything I heard. The Upper Arlington City Council consists of seven members, elected at large on a nonpartisan basis (i.e., there are no party primaries; anyone who wants to run in the general election can do so), for no more than two four-year terms. In 2019, three seats would be on the ballot, with the top three vote-getters being elected. The race was on.

Every step of the way made a big impact on me as a first-time candidate, starting with the collection of petition signatures. To get on the ballot for a city council election, a candidate must submit a petition signed by 50 to 150 registered voters. I collected signatures outside our main public library. Within minutes I was deeply moved by the way in which residents would take the time, while signing the petition, to share with me their thoughts about the city. It made me feel like a fiduciary to whom the people of Upper Arlington were entrusting their most sincere aspirations for our community. In a way I had not expected, that experience transformed my view of the responsibility of a public official. It turned out to be the first step in a process in which I became completely committed to the people whom I was seeking to serve.

Next came the campaign. The difficult part was the necessary adjustment to talking about myself. By that point I had spent nearly four decades at a law firm that prizes teamwork and disdains self-promotion. The sole focus is on the team's protection of the client's interests. Promotion of an individual lawyer's personal agenda is ordinarily intolerable. Suddenly, it became incumbent upon me, as a candidate, to deliberately draw attention to myself. I was taken aback the first time I saw the design of the campaign yard sign with my name emblazoned upon it in big letters. *What if someone from the firm sees this?* I thought—a laughable concern because many of my colleagues live in Upper Arlington. The competitive reality quickly kicked in, though, and overrode my anxiety.

One important lesson I had learned in the course of earlier campaigns for other candidates was that door-to-door, person-to-person canvassing makes a big difference. Not just in winning a campaign, but more importantly, it makes a difference in the campaigner. You cannot knock on doors day after day and not be transformed by what you hear, by the stories people tell you, and by understanding what their lives are like. It washes away any ideology, at least on a local level, where city government is delivering the fundamental services on which we all depend in our daily lives. We need the streets cleaned, the snow plowed, the leaves removed, sewer services, and traffic lights—all the things that are essential to give us the freedom to pursue our own objectives in life. Knocking on doors and, crucially, listening to fellow residents transforms a candidate as much as it transforms an electorate.

The campaign was intense but fun. Beginning shortly after the Fourth of July in 2019, I focused on door-to-door canvassing. My goal was to knock on every door (there are over fourteen thousand residences in Upper Arlington) on every street. I stopped swimming on weekday mornings, which was a big adjustment because I had become an almost-daily swimmer by that time, so I could get to work instead by six in the morning, then leave the office in time to knock on the first door by five in the afternoon. On weekends I would start at midday. Friends and family often accompanied me. In terms of sheer number of steps, no one outdid my longtime friend Brad Bradford, who became an almost daily companion on the door-to-door walks.

My family helped in many ways. I tried not to conscript them into any particular aspect because I did not want to impose campaign burdens upon them, but they always stepped up. When they have gone door to door, they have had the same moving experiences I have had in conversations with our fellow residents. They still talk about people whom they met and what they learned along the way. As a result, they have been able to see how impactful it is to learn from people who come from different walks of life. It is one thing to sit at home and assume what life is like for others, but when you actually get in touch with people, talking about real things, it gives a candidate a completely different view of the world. It provides a much more realistic lens on life—a world away from the often-dire news to which television and online news subject us.

It was a tremendous learning experience, far beyond anything I had expected. I knocked on every door along the way, despite the technically correct advice of political professionals to go only to the homes of people who statistically were more likely to vote for me. My reasoning in not using the likely-supporter lists was that there is something to learn from everyone, and I would be serving everyone if elected, not just those who had supported me. Usually, someone opened the door at about one out of every four homes. Video doorbell cameras at many of the other homes made it possible to leave a brief video message.

When I scratched the surface of the community that way, I was surprised to find Upper Arlington is a far more complex suburb and collection of neighborhoods than I had imagined, and it defies the stereotypes sometimes associated with such communities. Statistics notwithstanding, one who goes door to door throughout the city as I have will find doors opened by residents from a wide array of incomes, races, national origins, religions, family structures, sexual orientations, occupations, and principal household languages. Much of that is due to the proximity of Ohio State, adjacent to the city limits.

The most wonderful thing was hearing about what people were doing, or had done, with their lives. Nearly every day there were several such conversations that were highly energizing. It was exhausting, especially in the torrid heat of July and August, but completely worthwhile. Earnest conversations are an inspiration that overcome such exhaustion and completely reaffirm your commitment to serving your constituents. It is uplifting to hear about people's lives. People in my community are generally self-effacing and modest, but as in other communities, they have done remarkable things.

I made it to almost every door on almost every street in 2019. (Upper Arlington is slightly bigger than I had imagined, as a practical matter.) Something went right because I managed to come in first out of the five candidates on Election Day, with the top three being elected.

I speak from the dais of the Upper Arlington City Council chamber, 2023.

Serving for the Common Good

The first two years of the four-year city council term were dominated by the COVID-19 pandemic. Within weeks of my taking office, the pandemic dislocated the lives of nearly everyone in the world. We took it seriously. COVID-19 was the third leading cause of death in Upper Arlington during the first year of the crisis. The first order of business was to triage the municipal budget, identify the absolutely essential services, and determine what the city should be doing to protect residents from the contagion.

The City of Upper Arlington was one of the few cities that opened its public pools during the first summer of the pandemic, with some adaptations for public safety. We knew the pools would operate at a deficit that summer but decided that if there ever was a time to take such an extraordinary step, that was one. The public response was overwhelmingly positive. I would hear people emerge from the pool that summer saying things like "I don't know what I would do without this" and "For once, I am glad to be paying my city taxes."

One of my failures during the pandemic was my inability to convince my colleagues and the city administration that the city should provide some sort of direct stipend to the many individuals who had to "work from work" to keep our economy functioning locally. I will always remember the terrified look in the eyes of an older woman working as a grocery store cashier who told me in the early days of the pandemic, when it was unclear how risky it was to be out in public, that she had no choice but to show up for work every day at the store, where she was in constant contact with yet-unmasked customers in the checkout line. Life could not have gone on as it did without the involuntary courage of that lady and other people like her.

My proposal was that the City, which receives substantial income tax revenues, should send a rebate in a material amount ($250–$500, for example) to everyone other than City employees who had taxable income within a certain range ($10,000–$50,000, for example) from jobs at which they worked that year in the City of Upper Arlington. In the end the City established a fund from which to double match any bonus local employers paid employees who had come to work during the pandemic. It was not as robust a program as I had hoped the City would adopt, but it at least was some form of acknowledgement of the debt we all owe to that grocery store cashier and others who had no choice but to face the risks from which many people were better able to shelter themselves.

On a more constructive note, the pandemic provided an opportunity to walk each of the city's twenty-three public parks with family and fellow council members. It was productive to learn more about the parks that way and see so many people using them.

Fortunately for all, things gradually returned to normal in Upper Arlington and elsewhere. The city council agendas, in turn, became more routine once again. One big adjustment for me was learning how to engage in dialogues with my colleagues about their proposals and views in a tactful way, compared to the more direct approach to which I was accustomed after forty years in courtrooms and depositions. Advice from a few experienced appellate judges as to how they reason with their colleagues on three-judge panels was helpful, and I am still trying to do better.

It was fascinating in the process of the first four years to learn the details of operating an entity as complex as a city—everything including police and fire protection, parks and recreation, zoning and planning, street repair and maintenance, water and sewer service, snow removal, leaf collection, and many other municipal activities. Just as gratifying has been the ability to get things done for our residents. It makes my day to receive emails with messages like "Thanks, John, for your help with the downed wires" and "John, you've been so helpful with the Lane Road traffic situation" and "I cannot thank you enough, John, for the effort and work you put in regarding the speed limit signs on Sandover Road. It will make more of a difference than you will ever know."

On the other hand, I also had to learn how to take the heat for decisions some did not like. Almost every decision will please some and disappoint others. One particularly controversial issue involved the necessary replacement of the city's aging clay-court tennis facility, which had grown over time to twelve courts and was deteriorating. When projected costs rose to the extent that the budget would allow for a new facility with only nine courts, many avid tennis players became actively engaged in an intense dialogue with the city council. Nearly all the conversations were vigorous, informative, and civil. Some were not quite so measured and instead bordered on threats. It is all part of the process, but at least in the context of our city, encounters like those were the exception and did nothing to change my mind.

Heckling and abusive rhetoric are also easier to take because, in every vote on the city council, I have had the luxury of simply voting for what I believed was right. There were no other constraints on my judgment due to pressures from special interests, political parties, or contributors.

To keep our elections free from interference in Upper Arlington, I won majority support for a poll worker protection ordinance. We stepped up the penalties for threats to poll workers and disruption of the voting process. My friend Jason Dolin, a longtime lawyer, had the foresight to suggest and prepare an initial draft of the ordinance. It became a model ordinance that several other Ohio cities used for adoption of their own such legislation within a few weeks of its passage in Upper Arlington.

The hours of a city council member can sometimes be long, and the pay is nominal ($3,000 per year, plus a small supplement for purposes of the Ohio Public Employees Retirement System). But the satisfaction of serving people to whom I feel completely committed and a community that its residents take seriously has been enormous. When my colleagues and I have differed on issues, it has almost always been because we have different perspectives on what is important to the people of Upper Arlington. Fortunately for the common good, our disagreements have never been partisan or personal.

I loved the first four years of experience on the city council so much that I ran for reelection in 2023. The campaign followed the same plan, with the emphasis again on trying to knock on every door. The focus of the campaign was the consensus that, as one woman on Welsford Road put it, "This is an exciting time to live in Upper Arlington." She was right. The city's population was growing once again after sliding for several years. The city had issued permits for nearly $1.1 billion of new construction and renovation over the previous four years. A new $85 million community center was going up (the largest above-ground investment ever by the City of Upper Arlington). The larger parks and busier roads had received major upgrades. There were many new sidewalks and better zoning and development standards. The city had retained its AAA bond rating.

*During my reelection campaign for the Upper Arlington
City Council, I stop to take a photo in Northam Park
with the city symbol: the golden bear*

With the help of a vigorous campaign and the positive direction of the city, I won reelection. I came in first and, buoyed by turnout for a reproductive rights issue also on the ballot, was fortunate enough to get more votes than any other city council candidate in the history of the city in a contested election since the adoption of the City Charter in 1956—encouragement from my fellow residents I greatly appreciated and an opportunity to continue serving the people of Upper Arlington until January 2028. The strong vote of confidence was gratifying. But the most exciting feature was that so many people cared enough about the city to vote in the city council election.

Priorities on City Council

Due to the positive difference they have made for me and in the lives of many other residents, the city facilities about which I am most passionate are the swimming pools—so much so that some people in the municipal building evidently have given me the nickname John "Poolewicz." Anything that underscores the importance of the pools is fine by me. My primary goal on the city council is for every child in Upper Arlington to know how to swim by age five. Our community has thirty-seven thousand people, with three outdoor public pools plus one new indoor public pool. That is a favorable ratio in terms of pool capacity and population, certainly in comparison to other similar-sized cities.

Drowning is the leading cause of accidental death among children. Each death is ordinarily avoidable if children just know how to remain calm and float if they fall into the water. That is a minimum requirement. Ideally, children will also learn how to swim. We are in the enviable position of having the facilities to teach all the children of our city—and to establish a model for the entire nation—without spending a penny more on new pools, so it behooves us to maximize what we can do to allow every child in the city to learn to swim by age five.

The City of Upper Arlington has a comprehensive swimming-lesson program in place now. In the summer of 2024, it was available for 153 sessions with 620 children, which is great. The downside is the lessons can be given only in the mornings, generally between eight and nine thirty, which means a parent must be involved to take the child to the pool and either wait there or come back for pick up. Especially in single-parent or two-wage-earner households, that often becomes impractical. As a result, we can reach only a limited part of the population right now.

However, the city has just opened a new community center. It includes a four-lane, twenty-five-yard pool with a shallow end, which will provide the ability to offer swimming lessons at many more hours of the day and all year round. That will increase the swim-lesson capacity. Once that facility is running, getting the program up to speed will become primarily a staffing issue. Assuming my colleagues on the city council agree, and with the support of the Upper Arlington Schools, we will simply need to devote modest financial resources from the city budget to hiring enough instructors and lifeguards to make the program possible. We recently took a strong first step in that direction, with a $750,000 commitment to funding a new after-school water safety program for kindergartners.

Public safety through outstanding police and fire services has also been one of my highest priorities on the city council. Our home alarm went off in the middle of the night many years ago. I jumped out of bed, quickly got our children into our bedroom, secured the door, then called 911 as soon as the phone line freed up from the overriding call to the security system. I told the dispatcher what was happening. She said, "Sir, can you hold the line for just a moment?" I said okay. She came back within about thirty seconds and said, "Sir, the officer is in your backyard." Police response time that fast is priceless in any emergency, and we deeply appreciated it under the circumstances. (To our further relief, as it turned out, the alarm had gone off because a bug had gotten into a motion detector.)

Police, fire, and EMT response times are the essence of public safety and security in any city. The Upper Arlington Fire Department, for example, has an average response time of four minutes and forty-eight seconds, which is outstanding. When I learned in my first budget process on the city council that there were six unfilled budgeted positions on the police force, I made it a priority to make sure those positions were filled as soon as the training and certification processes could be completed. Ride-along time with our police officers and emergency medical technicians has allowed me to better appreciate all that goes into fast response times and confirmed the value the residents place on making that extraordinary service the norm.

Property tax relief and affordable senior housing have been other major issues. When I was canvassing during the 2023 election campaign, there was an older woman, a widow, standing on her doorstep, almost in tears, perplexed about her ability to pay the potentially rising property taxes. The homes in Franklin County had just been through a triennial reassessment, and taxes were subject to going up for all homeowners. The lady was genuinely anguished about how she was going to be able to make the next property tax payment. She had lived in the city virtually her whole life. Her children are here, and she did not want to have to move, but with the new taxes, she might have to do so. Many other residents have expressed the same sentiments. When I hear things like that, it opens my mind. *Is there something systematically in the law we could change? It shouldn't be like that. What can we do to help her?*

At one of our meetings not long afterward, the city council started talking about housing in the city. It is a huge topic. Property tax relief and housing—especially affordability—are key factors for so many people. On the city council, we are making an effort to understand what that involves and why housing is becoming less affordable. What can the city do about it? What difference, if any, would a municipal investment make? And are there ways to motivate the private sector to turn out quality homes at a more affordable price for people? These are not questions we have enough information to answer right now, but the discussion is a start.

One aspect of the community in which I unexpectedly have taken an avid interest is solid-waste recycling and food composting. I had a transformative experience with our solid-waste policy in 2024. It is an issue everywhere, of course, but we have a huge landfill here in central Ohio, and whatever goes in there is never going to go away. Until recently, going back millennia, nearly everything people had in their lives was biodegradable. The Greeks, the Romans, the other ancient peoples—almost everything they had was composed of natural materials. They did not have to worry as much about their garbage because it was all going to degrade anyway. But over the last few hundred years, especially since the beginning of the Industrial Revolution, we have started making products that are never going to break down. It is a particular problem with iron and steel and petrochemical derivatives and all the different types of plastics. We have all these used objects—metal parts, mattresses, plastic bags, tires—and they have to go somewhere, but we have only a finite amount of room.

As I see it, that is a major barrier to the well-being of our civilization. If we get to the point where we cannot manage any more waste, then population growth would become untenable. It is also a matter of our responsibility as stewards of the Earth.

There is a solution. I recently spent time at the local landfill site with another council member and others from the city administration, accompanied by a landfill spokesperson. As we watched the endless stream of trucks delivering mountains of waste to what is becoming a burgeoning wall one hundred feet high, the spokesperson reminded us that "74 percent of this could be diverted into recycling or composting." We must recycle and compost what we can because we otherwise will run out of room. We are currently and needlessly condemning huge tracts to be an eternal landfill. In three thousand years, it is still going to be there as our legacy. I want to call people's attention to that and to the advanced recycling and composting facilities we now have at our disposal. Avoidable accumulation of waste is a bigger actual threat to our civilization in many ways than a lot of the things we talk about in modern political dialogue.

Years ago, I thought that recycling was simply something good to do and that Maryline and I were just being good citizens by engaging in that process; I never completely understood why. Now I do. We can save three-quarters of the land we are condemning if we recycle and either resell, repurpose, or reuse waste or turn it into biofuel. I want to be able to convey to people why this is important, and I believe once people understand, they will do it, and they will do even more if it is easy for them. Then, of course, we must rethink our consumer culture too, because everything that is bought has to go somewhere, and we need to show the Earth a lot more respect than we have in the past.

The problems can seem tough, but they are not an "intractable reality" we need to "domesticate," in the words of Professor Ackerman. We can resolve them. The worst thing would be to do nothing at all. Hence my sincere appreciation for the opportunity to serve the people of Upper Arlington on the city council.

Chapter 11:
Family

Having opened this book with details of the family that brought me into the world, allow me to conclude with the story of the beloved family whom life has given to me.

The Woman Who Thought I Did Not Notice Her

Maryline and I first met in 1983. She was working in Columbus as a deputy director for the Ohio secretary of state, after having served at the Statehouse as a legislative aide to a member of the Ohio General Assembly. She volunteered for Senator John Glenn's presidential campaign while I was campaigning for Senator Hart. There was a Democratic Monday Lunch Club that met once a month in downtown Columbus. One particular Monday when Maryline attended, the speakers included representatives of candidates for the Democratic presidential nomination, including Senator Glenn, former Vice President Mondale, and Senator Hart.

I spoke for Senator Hart, and Maryline (who must have had a low bar for entertainment at the time) later told me she thought I was funny and cute. I told a true story that the Hart campaign was in such an obscure and underdog position at that early stage that when one would-be volunteer called the Ohio Democratic Party to ask for contact information, she was given the phone number for Harts department store. (There used to be a chain of stores in the Midwest called Harts.) Our conscientious state Democratic chair, James M. Ruvolo, also in attendance at the luncheon, did not think it was funny or cute when I told that story.

For over a year after that, Maryline and I would sometimes see each other on the street and stop and talk. She tells me she would smile as she walked away, thinking I had no idea who she was. She was wrong about *that*.

The next summer, in 1985, Maryline called for advice. She was interested in working in Washington, DC, and because I knew people from my political engagement and legal work, she thought I might be able to help. She asked if I would meet for coffee. We had dinner instead. There were no relevant names I could give her for the areas in which she wanted to work, so the conversation moved on to other topics.

I left the next day on a two-week trip to Russia, Belarus, and Ukraine (through the Seymour Plan for international travel at the firm), and while I was there, my mind kept circling back to her. I was supposed to be concentrating on learning about law in the Soviet Union through meetings with judges and lawyers from those areas. But I could not stop thinking about her. She is a beautiful woman with a lively spirit and engaging presence. It hit me at the right moment just how much I hoped she would not move to Washington. As soon as I returned, I called her, and the rest is history.

Maryline's Parents: Billy Barton and Pierre Michel

Maryline was born in France. Her mother, Billy Marie Andrée Hillone Barton, was Catholic and raised in the village of Decize, near Nièvre in the Loire Valley. She was the daughter of a rural French mother who married an American soldier serving in France during World War I. Maryline's father, Pierre S. Michel, was Jewish and came from Paris, where he was a successful entrepreneur. Billy and Pierre met during World War II in Paris. Billy had moved there around age twenty, working briefly in a light bulb factory while getting started on a career as a couturier, making and selling dresses designed to the specific requirements and measurements of the client. She had a special talent for garment and fabric cutting and maintained a boutique called Robbill (an amalgamation of the word *robe*, which means "dress" in French, and her first name) on the Rue de Sèze, near the Place de la Madelaine. She also worked as a model.

Billy's wartime memories included not only the hardships of living in the city under Nazi occupation but also a confrontation with two German soldiers at a sidewalk café. They asked her who she thought was going to win the war. She looked them in the eye and defiantly said, "The Americans!" She also gratefully remembered and often fervently recounted the emotional day in August 1944 when the American troops came through Paris as part of the liberation. In later years her patriotism for the United States was unparalleled.

Pierre Michel was a handsome businessman who, as a Jew, was wary on a daily basis of encounters with the Nazi occupiers (sometimes not wary enough, Billy feared at the time). He and Billy met when she was modeling. Eventually, he would sell the clothing Billy designed and made in her studio. Together, they prospered. After the war, they married and were successful in their business; lived in a fashionable building on the Avenue de Wagram, near the Etoile and the Arc de Triomphe; and took frequent trips to Cannes on the Cote d'Azur, where they mixed with movie stars and other luminaries, including Maurice Chevalier, Sidney Poitier, Errol Flynn, the Aga Khan of Pakistan, and Prince Phillip.

Then things changed. Gambling losses by Pierre at the horse track devastated the family's resources, and the marriage fell apart. Maryline, who had been born in Paris to Billy and Pierre as their second child, came to the United States in the late 1950s, when she was very young. Her mother emigrated with her, her older sister Dominique, and her younger brother William, despite a lack of English fluency and a scarcity of money.

Motivated by a vision of coming to America, Billy arrived by boat in New York with three young children, three suitcases, and $25 in her purse. She made her way with her children to Middletown, Ohio, where her mother had gone for medical treatment after World War II and where her father and two brothers, Roy and William Barton, who had left France in due course after the war, remained after her mother died. It was a huge decision and a significant risk. At the time, being a single parent was conspicuous, and being a single parent in a new country in which she did not know the language was even more precarious.

Pierre remained in Paris. He died alone there in the 1980s and was buried in a communal grave. During our sabbatical in Paris in 1991, Maryline tracked down his remains and had them reinterred separately with a tombstone.

Billy lived to be one hundred and one, worked long hours as a hair stylist and model, and eventually became fluent in English, which she graced with an enduring French accent. She stayed in Middletown for the rest of her life and married Judge John T. Lamb. Looking back at age one hundred, she told a local newspaper reporter, "You have to make decisions that are best for your kids. I will do whatever for them. All that mattered to me was my three kids." The mayor of Middletown paid tribute to her as a centenarian whose "life story of strength and determination stands as a hallmark for others to emulate and as an inspiration to others to pursue their dreams for themselves and their families." To the end she remained remarkable for her beauty, which led the celebrant of her funeral Mass to confess he once mistook a photograph of Billy Michel Lamb for a portrait of Elizabeth Taylor.

Maryline's Childhood and Formative Years

Maryline's upbringing was fun for her (with the continued language challenges faced by her mother being a source of mutual amusement) but hardly in the conventional mold of the standard American family structure of the late 1950s and early 1960s. In Paris and in Middletown, Maryline grew up in the French culture, which influenced much of who she is today. Her parents' divorce, their sudden impoverishment, and her immigration to the United States thrust her into circumstances that were unusual in her new community. Maryline became a naturalized citizen of the United States on March 17, 1969—a momentous occasion she has been able to relive several times when federal judges in Columbus have invited her to serve as guest speaker at local naturalization ceremonies.

Maryline graduated from Middletown High School. After an uphill battle by her and her sister Dominique to convince their mother of the value of a college education in the United States, she enrolled at Miami

University in Oxford, Ohio, following in the footsteps of Dominique. Through a Pell Grant, loans, summer jobs, and her mother's dedication, she was able to secure a college education. She worked at a variety of jobs, including waitressing and cleaning homes. After graduating with a bachelor of science in education, she taught math for six years at Weisenborn Middle School in Huber Heights, Ohio. But she always loved government and politics and left her job as an educator to move to Columbus and work in the state government. That was where she was working when we both were volunteering for our respective favorite Democratic presidential candidates.

From an early age, Maryline has had much the same values as I have sought to live by. Her step-grandmother was an Irish American Catholic who made sure the three grandchildren were at Mass every Sunday and received the sacraments of holy communion and confirmation. She also was a Democrat. In 1960, when the family was living in Middletown, a Republican bastion, Maryline's step-grandmother was in charge of the luncheon being prepared for then-Senator John F. Kennedy, who was running for president, at the Manchester Hotel. She took Maryline to the ballroom where he was going to be speaking with local Democrats, sat her in a chair, and said, "The next president of the United States is going to be sitting in this chair tomorrow." Maryline never forgot it.

Nor did Maryline overlook the racial prejudice she sometimes saw while growing up. She and her family had not seen racism in France during the 1950s. Witnessing it in the United States, combined with her own apprehension about being a newcomer with divorced parents, little money, and a different native language, strengthened Maryline's lifelong commitment to helping those who are marginalized and in need of support, reinforcing her belief in the importance of compassion and equality.

Our Marriage

After we had dated for a while, I knew Maryline was the woman with whom I wanted to spend the rest of my life. I asked if she wanted to take dancing lessons but did not tell her why. She agreed, and we learned a few dances, and then—after I proposed—I admitted I thought it would be useful for our wedding reception. Luckily, she said yes. We were each in our mid-thirties, and it was a great opportunity to gather family and friends. Maryline had not met many of my law school friends. I was sure she would like them, as she did.

We were married in the fall of 1987 in Columbus, at a nuptial Mass at which Father Kevin J. Kavanagh officiated at St. Joseph Cathedral. Just twelve days before the wedding, I was one of the lawyers at a banker's deposition. A cyclical collapse of the US stock market was unfolding as the deposition proceeded. The news got worse by the hour. It was a worrisome time. Luckily, it did not end up affecting our wedding plans in any material way. We had already booked and paid for most of it and did not have significant enough finances to be much disturbed by external events.

Thanks to savings, we were able to take a short honeymoon trip to Rio de Janeiro, inspired by my brief transit through Brazil seven years earlier on the way back from Africa. We stayed at a small hotel on the Copacabana Beach that my friend Peter Canfield had recommended. When coming back into the hotel from the beach one morning, it was a pleasant but complete surprise to find my law firm's managing partner, John Elam, and his wife Ginny and another couple on their way out. Since John always preached to his law partners that "the law firm partnership is like a marriage," and I was then a new partner, the coincidental encounter on our honeymoon amused me as an unintended effort on his part to make sure I understood that proposition.

Life with Maryline and Our Children

Maryline has had a demanding career. We have very much been partners as working parents. After starting as a teacher and then working for the state government in Columbus, she joined the admissions office at Ohio State. With the benefit of that experience, she took a job as director of admissions at The Wellington School, one of the three independent schools in Columbus. She held that position for nineteen years, long enough to have admitted the entire student body, which was a source of great satisfaction and success for her. Recently, she and Tracy Sullivan, a savvy woman from Boston, set up a college admissions guidance counseling service, College 101 Admissions Consultants LLC, which assists students with the college admissions process and continues to grow every day. Two of the most important women in my life—my wife and my mother—thus have been deeply passionate about fostering quality education.

We have been blessed with two children—Adam, who was born in August 1989, and Abigail, who was born in August 1993.

My family (Abigail, Maryline, and Adam) and I pose in our formal wear at a wedding in Colorado, May 2024.

It was fortunate my law firm was family friendly because the children always came first. Working for a law firm is intense. When Maryline and I began dating, we would often meet downtown, where she was working, and have dinner once or twice a week. On the nights we did not meet, I would call when I got home from work, around eleven or eleven thirty. That improved a little when we were married, and I made an effort to get home earlier, but it was still late; that was the culture and the expectation. Once we had children, both our lives changed. Without even much discussion, we both assumed we would be equal participants in raising them. Maryline also was working full-time, so we juggled our schedules to make it work. When there were two children to get out the door, one of us ordinarily would take one to the sitter while the other did the school run.

We also shared pickup responsibilities at the end of the day. That was equally hectic but ordinarily went well, with one exception. One afternoon in June 1994, when Maryline was indisposed, I picked up both Adam (who was almost five at the time) and Abigail (who was still a babe in arms). We had to stop at a state government office building on the way home. While we were going up the elevator, the governor of Ohio, George V. Voinovich, got on and rode with us until we reached the floor to which he was headed. I introduced him and Adam and Abigail to each other, then the door opened, and the governor and his security detail got off. The door closed, and Adam apparently had gotten off too, which I did not notice until it was too late. I was distraught at the thought of little Adam by himself in the gigantic building—and even more so by how I was going to explain that situation to Maryline. We got back to the level on which the governor had exited the elevator. When the door opened, there was Adam having a private conference with Governor Voinovich.

I thanked the governor on the spot for his kindness and delivered a follow-up note the next day. He responded in a thoughtful letter in which he wrote that Adam "is a very bright boy and, if you don't mind, he reminds me of my son George at that age. I couldn't get over Adam." The conversation may have had more of an impact on Adam than I realized at the time. As he has grown up, Adam has developed Republican inclinations, which would have warmed the GOP heart of Ohio's sixty-fifth governor.

If either of the children were sick, Maryline usually would stay home in the morning, and I would take over in the afternoon. We rarely missed any occasion at their schools. Whether it was a speech, an athletic event, or a performance during the school day, in the evening, or on the weekend, we both tried to be there. Maryline was particularly insistent about that; as the child of a single parent, she knew how it had felt when her mom was unable to attend school concerts or other events because she was working so hard. For both of us, work was necessary, and we valued our professional lives, but the children always came first.

Maryline and I were both lucky to have family help; my parents and her mother were nearby and could assist on many occasions. My parents were living in Columbus. Maryline's mother was only about one hundred miles away, in Middletown. As grandparents, they all enjoyed being involved in helping to raise Adam and Abigail. Grandparent duties generally consisted of coming over and watching the children when we had to be out or letting us bring them to their homes. It was a good way for the grandchildren and the grandparents to get to know each other outside the presence of the parents. It also gave Adam and Abigail a better understanding of their wider family and a different perspective on their own parents.

When the time came, we sent our children to independent schools, Adam to Columbus Academy and Abigail to The Wellington School—institutions that would challenge their thinking and help them to think for themselves. The school selections were a compromise. Several years earlier, on the trip to India, I had met a group of remarkable young students from the Doon School early one morning aboard a train in Uttar Pradesh. The boarding school, in the foothills of the Himalayas, then drew students not only from India but also from around the world (especially the British Commonwealth). I was so impressed that I promised myself that if I ever had children, I would send them to the Doon School. I talked with Maryline about that aspiration before we were married. She failed to see the intrinsic virtue of sending our children, if any, on their own at an early age to a boarding school in a foreign country, especially one that was thousands of miles away. So the one "prenuptial agreement" we made was that I would drop that plan. When our children reached school age, we had the opportunity to enroll them in the local public school and parochial school, both of which were excellent. In a nod to my hope of providing them with an even wider horizon, we opted instead for the independent schools.

I had a daily reminder that it became a habit to repeat to Adam and Abigail as I was dropping them off at school or saying goodbye in the morning (and that Abigail keeps in writing above her desk): "Work hard, do your best, tell the truth, learn everything you can, and help others."

Traveling as a Family

Prioritizing our family was never something we had to explicitly discuss. Maryline and I have agreed on every major decision. We never had to weigh the pros and cons; we naturally seemed to be on the same page.

One such decision arose when Maryline's job with the Ohio secretary of state ended at the beginning of 1991 when Democratic incumbent Sherrod Brown lost his bid for reelection. At that point I had been with the law firm for ten years. It turned out to be an ideal time to go on a sabbatical under the firm's program for partners who had reached that milestone. It was a paid sabbatical; there would be no interruption in compensation during three months' time off. The only requirement was that the lawyer do something other than practice law with the firm. The timing was perfect. Maryline was between jobs, and I had just finished a case to which I had devoted exclusive attention for several months. Adam was eighteen months old and had no particular commitments. We decided to live in Paris for three months.

It was risky. Maryline was no longer as fluent in her native language, and I had only rudimentary abilities in spoken and written French. Adam was just a toddler, so we were conscious of taking him away from the routine pediatric care with which we were familiar in the United States. Additionally, Maryline was not sure if there would be a job for her when we got back; the Democrats had lost a lot of offices in the 1990 election, so she knew she would have to look for something new. Despite the uncertainty, one of Maryline's relatives found an apartment for us in Neuilly-sur-Seine, a suburb adjacent to Paris, and we decided we were ready to go.

Then, in January 1991, the Gulf War (Desert Storm) started in the Middle East. It kicked off just two weeks before our planned departure date. The firm was still supportive of our trip, but the general mood across the US was one of concern. However, we were prepared to take the risk, and we set off. Ominously, it seemed as if there were only a few dozen passengers aboard our transatlantic flight (we had almost an entire section to ourselves) because people were apprehensive about the possible complications of flying.

For three months, from February through April 1991, the three of us were together twenty-four hours a day, something we had never experienced. It went well, and we had a great time. We stayed mostly in Paris. Our daily routine was to have breakfast and get Adam ready. Then we would go outdoors and to the market to buy fresh meat and produce for lunch and dinner before stopping by a local playground. After lunch, we would pick a Metro stop, ride the train there, and take a long walk back, with Adam usually napping in the stroller. We ordinarily were home by around four, when the daily edition of *Le Monde* appeared on the newsstands. I would buy a copy and sometimes hand it to Adam, who would sit up in the stroller and look through it on the way back to our apartment, to the amusement of passersby. The daily fresh baguettes were ready for purchase by then too. We made occasional trips to places such as Normandy (including the D-Day beaches and American cemetery) in the north and Decize (the hometown of Maryline's mother and uncles) in the Loire Valley.

We loved our time in France and the opportunity to get to know the country better from a day-to-day perspective. We have been back many times. Beginning with the sabbatical, the significant time spent in France deepened Adam's links to one of his ancestral nations. Once he became an adult, he successfully went through the process of obtaining dual nationality with France on the basis of Maryline's birth to French parents in France.

We both value education a great deal and love history and travel, so it has been important to us to educate our children about the world. They each have been accustomed to travel from an early age. The first time all four of us traveled abroad was when Adam was in fourth grade and Abigail was in kindergarten. Every year after that, we tried to travel to a different country and would go to its museums, parks, historic sites, and religious buildings—churches, synagogues, mosques, whatever places of worship were prevalent in that country. Our premise was that we could better understand a nation's values by making an attempt to understand its religious faith and practices in comparison with our own. We would do the same sort of thing at home too. When Adam and Abigail were younger, we would frequently travel around Ohio on Sundays and go to local sites.

Wherever we were, we found something interesting to see or do. One time, when Adam and Abigail were quite young and the four of us were in Southern California, we visited the Richard Nixon Presidential Library and Museum. It is the official repository of significant memorabilia of the Nixon administration. The library had recently accessioned a large slab of the Berlin Wall. The children were too young to remember the fall of the Berlin Wall—Adam was only a few months old in November 1989—but we wanted them to have a sense of such important historical events. A docent escorted us around the museum. When we got to the chunk of the Berlin Wall, we could see and feel the tactile reality of the massive barrier the Soviets had installed to limit an exodus from East Berlin, which they controlled after World War II. The docent said, "This was part of the Berlin Wall." Adam started asking questions. "What was the Berlin Wall? Why was there a wall? What is communism? Why did they put up a wall?" We could see the docent light up at hearing the impact the artifact was having.

We were glad too. The night the wall was breached, people started pouring through. We were having dinner with several friends at our home and watched the event unfold on the television. You could feel the rush of freedom flowing. Even though we were thousands of miles away in the United States, Maryline and I knew it nonetheless would mean a better life for millions of people.

On another occasion, we had an even more poignant encounter with modern history. While driving through south-central Pennsylvania on the way to Washington, we stopped at the field outside of Shanksville where United Airlines Flight 93, the fourth plane in the 9/11 attack, crashed due to the courage of the passengers who seized control from the hijackers and valiantly averted an even larger tragedy. Their commandeered plane was supposedly heading for the White House, but the passengers overwhelmed the terrorists and brought the aircraft down far away from their intended destination.

The crash site is in the middle of rural Pennsylvania. As you come over a hill, you can see where the plane went down. When we visited, hundreds of cars were there, full of people who had come to remember and pray. This was within a year of the events of 2001. The tragedy was still fresh. A team from NBC News was there and asked to interview Abigail about what she was seeing. Not yet ten years old, she gave a heartfelt and thoughtful response on camera. The whole place is deeply moving—yet defiant. The passengers on the doomed plane were people who fought back with valor and saved the lives of countless others.

The events of September 11, 2001, had been a defining moment for our family and for all Americans. I was at work that morning, preparing to file a brief in federal court. Maryline was at her office. Adam and Abigail were at their schools. I was walking down a hallway back to my office shortly before nine. A colleague asked if I thought this meant war. I asked what he was talking about. He told me an airliner had just crashed into one of the World Trade Center towers in New York. I had a small television in my office. I turned it on immediately. Watching with several of my colleagues, I could hardly believe what was unfolding before our eyes. A second plane crashed into the other of the twin towers, then a third plane hit the Pentagon, and the fourth fell outside Shanksville.

There was a special noontime Mass in downtown Columbus that day at St. Joseph Cathedral, led by Bishop James A. Griffin, a remarkable leader who never failed to exude the sympathetic qualities of a parish priest. The church was already packed as I entered. At the end of the Mass, the congregation ardently sang "America the Beautiful" as tears rolled down many cheeks.

Adam and Abigail were in separate schools, so Maryline and I called from our offices to make sure they were okay. Each school had shared the news with the students calmly and professionally, and there was no need to rush to collect them. That was fortunate because it would have been difficult to get there quickly. A huge traffic jam clogged downtown

Columbus that morning, as nearly all offices quickly closed, and thousands of people left work to head home simultaneously.

We picked up Adam and Abigail that afternoon and went straight home to watch further reports on television. One unusual aspect of that afternoon was the silence in the sky. Our neighborhood is under one of the main flight paths into Port Columbus International Airport, so we are accustomed to hearing a steady stream of descending airplanes. But that day, all flights had been grounded. The usual procession of airplanes and jet noise disappeared. The one exception was the sound we heard in the late afternoon as the president's plane, *Air Force One*, flew low overhead a few miles to the north of Columbus, accompanied by a squadron of fighter craft. They were on their way to Washington on a diversionary path from Florida and Louisiana to Nebraska and then eastward.

As with all Americans who were alive at the time, we will never forget that day.

* * *

With Adam and Abigail, we have visited many remarkable places around the world (including Australia, Canada, China, France, Italy, Japan, Mexico, Morocco, Spain, Turkey, and the United Kingdom) as well as sites around the United States. On each of these trips, overseas and at home, we have tried to connect with as many people and day-to-day settings as we can. Each trip has exposed us to new experiences and walks of life and given us a new perspective on the world and a better sense of our own place in it. In addition to our international travels, we visited New York often when Adam and Abigail were young. Both Maryline and I wanted to instill the value of travel in our kids, and I believe we succeeded; we *still* travel a lot as a family.

I recently asked Adam why he thought travel was so important to us, and he said, "It allows you to make the world smaller and understand different places better by visiting them." He is right. The best way to understand an unfamiliar place is to go there, get lost, find your way around, become acquainted with the culture—whether it is partially familiar to begin with or entirely new—and soak up as much as possible. For my family and me, travel has been one of the best ways to nurture a love of learning and respect for history.

Although I am glad to lead the family on our travels, Maryline and I recognized early on we should give Adam and Abigail some level of responsibility too. We used to play a game in foreign cities called, for example, Lost in Paris or Lost in London. Abigail would suddenly get the assignment of figuring out how to find our way back to the hotel or go from one place to another. We started doing that when she was about six, and she loved leading us.

Abigail has maintained a high threshold for entertainment on our family travels. She would get bored and try to connect with other children for a more fun experience. She had seen me interacting with local residents in various places and happily stepped into that role herself. When we were in Japan, climbing Mount Fuji, for example, a large group of Japanese schoolchildren came along on the path with us, walking briskly and happily. She quickly befriended them. Snapping out of the slower pace of her indifference with us just moments before, she merrily set off with her new friends. She was never out of our sight but seemed to be having a good time with her Japanese contemporaries.

Over the years she has become friends with many different people. She is particularly fond of a photo taken of her in Hiroshima, which she believes reflects our willingness to expose her to new experiences and the realities of the world. During our family visit to the Hiroshima Peace Memorial Museum, we watched educational movies about the atomic bomb. The photo captures a group of Japanese children sitting and watching the film, with Abigail right in the middle, completely integrated.

A trip to China was especially eye-opening. In 2006 the four of us flew to Shanghai, where we stayed for several days, and then took the night train to Beijing. It was a wonderful adventure. Shanghai was astonishing; we could see it growing and changing around us even while we were there, and everything was done on such a mass scale. That trip taught us and our children that you make assumptions about places at your own peril. On the night train from Shanghai to Beijing, you can see out into the farm fields after daybreak. We had just come from the great opulence and momentum of Shanghai, in stark contrast to the rustic conditions we saw in the fields. When we arrived in Beijing, it was back to a different world.

We had a memorable experience in Shanghai while walking through a park when a young Chinese girl approached us. She asked, in English, if she could talk with us. She and our family had a lot of questions for each other about the lives we were leading. The most unforgettable exchange was when she asked, "What could I be if I came to America?" Immediately, and without coordination on our part, we all simultaneously responded, "Whatever you want to be!"—a spontaneous confirmation of the faith the four of us have in the opportunity life offers in the United States.

Before returning to the US, I was able to reach several Yale graduates in China, as I had done on such occasions when traveling elsewhere. We had two fascinating experiences as a result. One graduate was serving as a justice of the Supreme Court of China. He welcomed us to his chambers, where we had a lengthy conversation about the work of the court and international trade policy, in which he specialized. One of his staff members showed us around the inner rooms of the courthouse afterward. The other graduate served as president of the Yale Club of China. He offered to host us for dinner, an invitation we were honored and delighted to accept. His hospitality was extraordinary and gave us a glimpse of the upper echelons of Chinese society.

Family travel has always gone hand in hand with my love of languages. Maryline and I have always encouraged Adam and Abigail to pick up what they can, and they have seen the benefits of doing so on trips like the one to Japan. With a French-born mother, they have always had encouragement to learn French. When Adam was learning French at Tufts, he planned to study abroad for one semester of his junior year. However, during our discussions, it became clear that staying for a full year, not just a semester, would be more beneficial. Although especially tough for Maryline, who would miss him terribly, she appreciated that he would be learning her native language and spending time in her home city. So she agreed. We knew that being immersed in the culture for a whole year would be perfect for Adam, and it was. He ended up staying through the summer too, as he got an internship at the Louvre.

Adam became so proficient in French that he could speak it fluently by the end of his stay. When two of our friends were in Paris later, Adam went to their hotel to meet them. While waiting for them to come down, he spoke with the concierge in French so normally that, when the concierge later heard him speaking in English to our friends, he commented to them on how well Adam spoke English. Abigail is also competent in languages, when she chooses to be, even though she has not yet had the same immersive experience as Adam.

Together, we find wisdom in the observation, attributed to Charlemagne, that "when you learn another language, you gain another soul." In the process, you can perceive more clearly the soul with which you started. Despite our commonalities worldwide, societies and cultures are different. Learning languages is the first gateway to understanding those differences and reaffirming our own identity.

Parenting into Adulthood

We have raised our children to be hard workers and are proud of the adults they have become. Adam is now thirty-five and has lived in New York and London, where he has worked as a lawyer. Because Maryline had put her foot down about the Doon School in India, he went to elementary and secondary school in Ohio and then to Tufts University in Boston, from which he graduated with a bachelor's degree, magna cum laude, in French and art history. He had long wanted to work in New York and managed to secure a job at Christie's, the leading art auction house, as a specialist in European arts and sculpture. Competition for the role was stiff, but he succeeded and excelled there. So well, in fact, that one day, out of the blue, they asked if he would move to the London office. It was a big risk because it meant uprooting everything and starting again in a new city. But he managed it and spent several successful years there as a specialist in nineteenth-century articles.

He built a remarkable circle of friends in London and then returned to the US to study law at Boston University School of Law. After graduating, he passed the New York bar exam and began his job as an associate at a major international law firm, splitting his time between the New York and London offices. He now works as an associate at another prestigious global law firm. Maryline and I never pushed Adam toward law school, although we knew early on that he would excel in the legal profession.

Adam recently became engaged to Silvia Marroquin, a talented and lovely young woman who earned a bachelor's degree with a concentration in Latin American studies from Sciences Po Paris, a master in economic law from Sciences Po Law School, and a master of laws from Georgetown University Law Center. Silvia works as a lawyer in the arbitration of international commercial and investment treaty disputes and is fluent in five languages. We are all quite happy for Adam and Silvia and look forward to their life together.

Abigail is thirty-one. After The Wellington School, she also went east for her undergraduate studies, graduating from Connecticut College with a bachelor's degree in history and American studies, and then moved to Boston to work in the private sector. She was there for four years and resourcefully found several good positions at the TJ Maxx headquarters in Framingham and in a development capacity for Massachusetts General Hospital. Abigail returned to Columbus during the pandemic and took a job as an annual giving coordinator for the Mid-Ohio Food Collective. She is now (like her mother before her) a legislative aide in the Ohio General Assembly. It has been amazing to watch her take risks in her career too; she has great people instincts. She was born with excellent intuition and social skills. Even when she was little, she would make observations about people that left me wondering how she had such a mature understanding at such a young age. It was no surprise to Maryline and me when her classmates at The Wellington School elected her class president.

Especially because she has such a big heart, Abigail is flourishing in her legislative staff work with the Ohio General Assembly. Most impressively to Maryline and me, she applied for and obtained the staff position entirely on her own, without any prompting or help from either of us. It was through her own initiative that she took that risk—a risk that has promptly shown its rewards. In her first year on the job, working for a respected state legislator who has a special commitment to pediatric health care, Abigail's compassion has driven her naturally to discover and focus on the details of highly technical line items of the state government operating budget, such as Medicaid funding and the Ohio Fair School Funding Plan. She sees and understands the human impact of such budgetary decisions and the corresponding need to understand their financial intricacies so she can make a positive contribution to the legislative process as a legislative aide. She has a quick grasp of the lawmakers' interactions, thanks to her intuitive gifts, and respects the gravity and importance of the work in which the legislators are engaged. Abigail is especially fortunate as a legislative aide to be working with several highly talented legislators and fellow staff members of both parties.

One of our greatest joys is that after all these years, Maryline and I are still close to our children. Maryline speaks with them both daily, and I, too, am on the phone (or text or email) with each of them almost as frequently. We also try to keep up with technology. Abigail has been teaching us how to answer a FaceTime video call so it is not showing only our noses—and we are learning. She has a big job to do in keeping us current with terminology and technology.

Finding Balance

Working as a lawyer is demanding, with enormous time pressures. I had to figure out how to manage that. One thing I prioritized was getting home for dinner. Adam says he can count on one hand the times I was not at the dinner table when he was growing up. I am sure it was more than that, especially when I had to travel out of state, but I am glad he remembers it that way. Dinner was a family affair, even when we had dinners with friends and dignitaries. We wanted Adam and Abigail to participate in the conversation and welcomed their opinions as long as they could back up what they said with reasons.

As a lawyer, much of what I do must remain confidential, including from my family, under the attorney-client privilege. They have grown accustomed to this over the years, understanding there are limits on what I can share. In the early days of our marriage, it was an adjustment for Maryline and me. It became easier when we saw other professional couples dealing with the same frustration, understanding it was not a lack of confidence or unwillingness to share but a matter of the attorney-client privilege, under which a lawyer must not divulge confidential information a client shares for the purpose of seeking legal advice. It helped that my family was able to attend several court arguments I presented, giving them a look at what I do. Adam said recently he understood me better after about five minutes in law school because it occurred to him that the way I think about things, address issues, and formulate thoughts is closely related to the US legal education system.

As Adam and Abigail have grown older, they have often come to me or Maryline for advice. That has been much tougher. These issues have generally been about their work or personal relationships. It is challenging because we do not know as much as they do about the situation, and giving advice based on incomplete information is risky. Moreover, the world has changed much since Maryline and I were their ages, making it even more of a challenge to give good advice relevant to the era in which they are living. It is also harder when your children ask for advice because it is not a business relationship. Your children put extra weight on your response, making it difficult to be as clinical.

Abigail tells me she finds me to be a useful mediator. When she comes to me with an issue, I ask her to explain the problem, the solution, and her plan to address it. She knows I will not just hand her a solution but will counsel her to see both sides.

We have also had discussions about the value of mistakes. I am quite far from perfect and, like everyone else, make mistakes. I have tried to show Adam and Abigail that mistakes are not uncommon but that we should make them only once. Learn from them, and do not repeat them.

Chapter 12:
Second Wind

I have reached the age of seventy. Our law firm partnership agreement provides that a partner must exit at the end of the year when they attain that age. For me, the departure from the firm is a gateway to other opportunities, for which I feel as if I have gotten a second wind. I find great motivation in words of wisdom from a church service we attended at Christmas 2023 in London, where we spent the holiday with Adam. The homilist included in her sermon the adage of British writer Jeanette Winterson that "only the impossible is worth the effort"—a sentiment that has subconsciously guided me as long as I can remember. For seventy years now, I have focused much effort on the pursuit of dreams that were beyond my reach at their inception. The life I have lived as a result has been, for me, well worth the effort.

Achievement has its own satisfaction. None of my accomplishments, such as they are, have been unprecedented or otherwise unique to me. Yet for me, they each have been a completely positive experience. Each has involved substantial risk and hardship and provided much fulfilment and happiness. Freedom from self-consciousness has been the common denominator of all these experiences. When the goals are much larger than me, or initially beyond my reach, I forget about myself and instead focus on the objective. In such a context, disappointments, doubts, mistakes, and shortfalls along the way pale in comparison. For these reasons, as Langston Hughes so eloquently wrote, it is important to "hold fast to dreams, for when dreams go, life is a barren field frozen with snow."

I have been blessed with a family who has joined me in understanding the value of risk and the virtue of its reward. In sharing many of these experiences, we have found much satisfaction together. We each know we are likely to do better if we embrace the advice of Ralph Waldo Emerson to "always do what you are afraid to do," the insistence of Eleanor Roosevelt that "you must do the thing you think you cannot do," and the challenge of John F. Kennedy to choose goals "not because they are easy but because they are hard."

On March 15, 2014, almost a century to the day after my grandfather Joseph Kulewicz had arrived in New York in pursuit of his dreams, Maryline and I reserved part of the Ellis Island facility and invited our extended family and local friends to join us in marking the occasion. Several dozen people came together for a Saturday afternoon luncheon, followed by a short program. History is important, so I spoke about my paternal grandfather and the times in which he lived. We asked our guests to share their own observations about the experiences of their families. Our collective memories and reflections overflowed the gallery and the arrival hall beneath us.

It was awesome to look out at the room as I spoke. Standing there, I could see clearly how my grandfather's initiative had led to successive generations of opportunity and enriched the nation to which he had come one hundred years earlier. My paternal grandmother was equally responsible for that, as were my mother's ancestors who had come to America generations earlier from various points in England and Germany. The same is true of Maryline and her family, who moved to the United States from France in the postwar decades.

Looking around the room, I could literally see the fullness of life for the generations that have followed, now spanning a wide range of circumstances but, to a person, committed to the virtues of hard work, determination, and the pursuit of their dreams. We each could count an abundance of blessings.

At the end of the program, a young man rose and sang "The Impossible Dream." His eloquent voice filled the room, and the entire building, with not only nostalgia about our blessings but also the inspiration of how large the future can be for each of us if we dare to dream. As each reader knows from times when they have staked their life on what they have dreamed, the chances we take in life are what make all the difference.

The "successive generations" are all in attendance, along with many of our New York friends, to mark the one hundredth anniversary of my paternal grandfather's arrival at Ellis Island.